THE EVERYDAY QUIZ BOOK

Robert Duffy

POOLBEG

For Shona and Damien

First published 1993 by
Poolbeg
A division of Poolbeg Enterprises Ltd.
Knocksedan House,
123 Baldoyle Industrial Estate, Dublin 13

A catalogue record of this book is available from the British Library.

ISBN 1 85371 318 X

Cover illustration by Lawrence Griffin
Cover design by Poolbeg Group Services Ltd.
Set by Typeform Repro
Printed by The Guernsey Press Co. Ltd.
Guernsey, Channel Islands

Contents

Preface

The layout of this sixth Poolbeg Quiz Book is a lot different from the others. There are no topics, just pages and pages of questions and answers—and birthdays. People are always curious about what important things happened on their own birth date. If you were born on 18 June, for example, you were born on the anniversary of the Battle of Waterloo. This author has the same birthday as Queen Victoria and Bob Dylan. Anyway, this book is easy to follow: it starts with 1 January and ends 366 days later on 31 December. Every single day is represented, though some days are juicier than others. If you haven't got a question on your birth date, don't worry: your date will be covered in one of the birthday lists.

As the book was coming together, it became obvious that royal people and Pope people were fond of sticking Xs and Vs and Is after their names. These Roman numerals are a bit of a handful, so you will find a crash course on how to read Roman numerals just after the answers.

Another useful item stumbled upon was a chart for working out which day of the week any particular event fell on, or will fall on, between 1801 and 2000. If this appears complicated, get an adult to help you.

As usual, the latest Poolbeg Children's Quiz Book is more challenging than easy. Quiz books are about making it fun to learn.

JANUARY

1 January 1804
From which country did Haïti win its independence?

1 January 1958
Which important European organisation came into being on this date?

1 January 1959
Which communist leader overthrew the Batista government in Cuba?

1 January 1973
Which countries joined the European Economic Community (EEC) on this date?

> **Birthdays**
> 1 January 1735   Paul Revere, American patriot
> 1 January 1895   J. Edgar Hoover, Director of the FBI

2 January 1492
Which Queen of Spain (who later sponsored Christopher Columbus) captured the city of Granada from the Arabs?

3 January 1924
Which treasure-laden pharaoh's tomb was discovered by Howard Carter and the Earl of Caernarvon?

3 January 1959
Which territory became the forty-ninth state of the United States?

4 January 1986

Phil Lynnot, who died of a drug overdose on this date, was lead singer with which famous band?

Birthdays	
4 January 1603	Isaac Newton, scientist
4 January 1809	Louis Braille, blind teacher

5 January 1922

Which Irish-born explorer died suddenly on his way to the Antarctic?

5 January 1981

Who was charged with the "Yorkshire Ripper" murders?

6 January 1412

This is the birthday of which famous French soldier and saint?

6 January 1919

Which American president died first, Theodore Roosevelt or Franklin Roosevelt?

7 January 1844

Marie-Bernard Soubirous, born on this date, is now better known by what name?

7 January 1965

Which actor-comedian is best remembered as "Biddy Mulligan, the Pride of the Coombe"?

7 January 1975

Which Irish statesman's wife died on the eve of their sixty-fifth wedding anniversary?

8 January 1935

In which state was Elvis Presley born: Mississippi, Tennessee, or Alabama?

8 January 1947

David Jones is the real name of which British pop singer?

9 January 1913

Richard Nixon was born in which west coast state of the United States?

Birthdays
10 January 1945   Rod Stewart, pop star

---

11 January 1928

Who wrote *Far from the Madding Crowd* and *The Mayor of Casterbridge*?

12 January 1893

Hermann Göring was commander of Hitler's air force. What is the German name for the air force?

12 January 1976

Hercule Poirot's creator died on this date. Name the writer.

13 January 1941

In which city did James Joyce die?

14 January 1742

Which heavenly body, only visible every seventy-six years, was named after a British astronomer who died on this date?

14 January 1938

Which film was Walt Disney's first full-length cartoon?

15 January 1929

Which Black American civil rights leader won the Nobel Peace Prize in 1964?

16 January 1991

Which war began in the Middle East on this date?

17 January 1706

Which American statesman developed the lightning conductor?

17 January 1860

Who was the first President of Ireland?

17 January 1874

Twins Chang and Eng died on this date. What was special about them?

Birthdays

17 January 1899	Al Capone, Chicago gangster
17 January 1942	Mohammed Ali (Cassius Clay), boxer

---

18 January 1892

Half of the Laurel and Hardy team was born in England. Which of them was born in America on this date?

18 January 1912

Who led the second team to reach the South Pole?

Birthdays

18 January 1913	Danny Kaye, American comedian

---

19 January 1807

Who commanded the Confederate troops during the American Civil War?

19 January 1988

Which young handicapped writer won the 1988 Whitbread Book of the Year Award for *Under the Eye of the Clock*?

20 January 1936

Edward, Prince of Wales, became King Edward VIII of England on the death of his father in 1936. Which King George was Edward's father: George IV or George V?

Birthdays
20 January 1896   George Burns, American actor
20 January 1930   Buzz Aldrin,
                   second person on the Moon

---

20 January 1961

Who was the first Roman Catholic president of the United States?

20 January 1968

Ireland's first honorary citizen, who died on this date, has a library named after him in Ballsbridge, Dublin. Who was he?

20 January 1981

US embassy hostages were released in Tehran on the same day as the inauguration of which president?

21 January 1793

Which King Louis of France lost his head on this date?

21 January 1876

Which man, born in Liverpool, founded the Irish Transport and General Workers' Union?

21 January 1919

In which building in Dawson Street, Dublin, did the first Dáil Éireann meet?

21 January 1924

Which high-ranking Soviet communist died on this date?

21 January 1925

Which New York television policeman sucks lollipops?

21 January 1976

Which supersonic aircraft entered commercial passenger service with flights from London to Bahrein and from Paris to Rio de Janeiro?

22 January 1901

This woman's death marked the end of an era. Who was she?

22 January 1940

Which English actor played Birdy in *The Field* and the title role in *The Elephant Man*?

23 January 1989

Salvador Dali, famous for his pictures of melting clocks and other surreal images, was a native of which country?

24 January 1848

What did James Marshall discover in California?

24 January 1965

Who was the first non-royal British citizen to receive a state funeral?

Birthdays
24 January 1941   Neil Diamond, American singer

---

25 January 1759
Who is considered to be Scotland's national poet?

25 January 1874
Who wrote *Liza of Lambeth*, *The Razor's Edge*, and several
other novels and short stories?

25 January 1947
Which former gangster died penniless in Florida?

26 January 1788
Which country celebrated its bicentennial in 1988?

Birthdays	
26 January 1880	Douglas MacArthur, Second World War US general

26 January 1907
The controversial play *The Playboy of the Western World*
opened at the Abbey Theatre and there were riots outside.
Who wrote the play?

Birthdays	
26 January 1908	Stephane Grapelli, jazz violinist
26 January 1925	Paul Newman, actor

27 January 1756
In which Austrian city was Mozart born?

27 January 1832
Charles Lutwidge Dodgson was the real name of which
famous children's writer?

27 January 1868
With what words did Henry Morton Stanley greet David Livingstone?

27 January 1967 (a)
Name the first solo round-the-world yachtsman, who was knighted on this date.

27 January 1967 (b)
Which Apollo rocket went on fire on its launch pad, killing Gus Grissom, Edward White, and Roger Chaffee: *Apollo 1, Apollo 2,* or *Apollo 3*?

28 January 1841
In which country was explorer Henry Morton Stanley born?

28 January 1939
Ireland lost one if its greatest poets on this date. Who was he?

28 January 1986
How was American schoolteacher Christa MacAuliffe killed?

29 January 1879
Which famous American comedian and actor had the first names William Claude?

30 January 1649
Who ruled England after King Charles I was beheaded?

30 January 1933
Who was appointed Chancellor of Germany by Paul von Hindenburg?

30 January 1948
Which man of peace was assassinated in New Delhi?

30 January 1972
Thirteen civilians were killed by British soldiers in which Irish city?

> **Birthdays**
> 30 January 1860   Anton Chekhov, Russian writer
> 30 January 1931   Gene Hackman, American actor

31 January 1943
The German army finally surrendered after failing to capture which Russian city?

31 January 1951
Name the Genesis drummer and solo singer who played the title role in the film *Buster*.

FEBRUARY

1 February
This is the feast day of which Irish saint?

1 February 1901
Who played the part of Rhett Butler in the film *Gone with the Wind*?

1 February 1966
Star of *The General* and other silent film classics, this comic actor never successfully made the switch to talkies. Who was he?

1 February 1979
Who returned to Iran to lead the country after the Shah had been deposed?

2 February 1665

What name did the English give to New Amsterdam after they took it from the Dutch?

2 February 1709

Alexander Selkirk, rescued by Woodes Rogers from the Juan Fernández Islands on this date, was probably the inspiration for which fictional character?

2 February 1989

Soldiers from which neighbouring country finally left Afghanistan on this date?

Birthdays
2 February 1882   James Joyce, Irish writer

---

3 February 1468

Who was the first person outside China to develop the movable-type printing press?

3 February 1907

Who wrote *Hawaii, Space, Centennial*, and other blockbuster novels?

4 February 1868

What was Constance Markievicz's maiden name?

4 February 1902

The *Spirit of St Louis* was the name of the plane used by which famous aviator?

4 February 1945

Churchill, Roosevelt and which Soviet leader held a peace conference at Yalta?

5 February 1945
Reggae singer Bob Marley was a native of which Caribbean country?

5 February 1989
Which satellite television company was launched on this date?

6 February 1952
When King George VI of England died, his daughter Elizabeth was visiting which east African country?

6 February 1958
A plane crash in Munich resulted in the death of seven soccer players. To which English club did they belong?

Birthdays
6 February 1895   George "Babe" Ruth, baseball player

7 February 1867
What kind of transport system did Carlow-born William Dargan help to build?

Birthdays
7 February 1812   Charles Dickens, English writer
7 February 1911   Ronald Reagan,
                   American actor and politician
8 February 1925   Jack Lemmon, American actor

8 February 1587
Which queen signed the death warrant for Mary Queen of Scots?

8 February 1931
Which actor, noted for his rebel image, starred in only three films: *East of Eden, Rebel Without a Cause,* and *Giant?*

9 February 1923
Which famous Irish playwright spent time in jail and wrote *Borstal Boy?*

9 February 1926
Which economist, who worked for Aer Lingus, became leader of Fine Gael and subsequently Taoiseach?

9 February 1969
Which large Boeing aircraft had its first test flight on this date?

9 February 1983
Which valuable racehorse was kidnapped from Ballymany Stud, near Droichead Nua (Newbridge), Co. Kildare?

10 February 1837
Aleksandr Pushkin was killed in a duel at the early age of 37. What nationality was he?

10 February 1840
Albert, son of the Duke of Saxe-Coburg-Gotha, married his first cousin in 1840. Who was his famous wife?

10 February 1913
The remains of which British explorer were found over a year after he had managed to reach the South Pole?

Birthdays	
10 February 1930	Robert Wagner, American actor
10 February 1847	Thomas Edison, American inventor
11 February 1936	Burt Reynolds, American actor

11 February 1847

Who was the first person to record "Mary Had a Little Lamb"?

11 February 1990

Name the leader of the African National Congress who was released from a South African prison in 1990.

12 February 1809 (a)

Which American president was born in a log cabin in Kentucky?

12 February 1809 (b)

Which nineteenth-century scientist put forward the theory of evolution?

13 February 1542

Catherine Howard, who was beheaded on this date, was the wife of which King of England?

14 February 1779

Which English seaman set out on his third trip to the Pacific in 1776 but never returned?

14 February 1929

Which gangster is alleged to have ordered the infamous St Valentine's Day Massacre?

14 February 1944

Who directed the films *Bugsy Malone, Fame,* and *The Commitments*?

14 February 1945

Which elegant German city was devastated by Allied bombers less than three months before the ending of the Second World War?

14 February 1981

In which Dublin suburb did the Stardust disaster happen?

15 February 1564

Which Italian astronomer was imprisoned by the Inquisition for declaring that the Earth moved round the Sun?

15 February 1942

Which strategic city fell to the Japanese on this date?

Birthdays

15 February 1874   Ernest Shackleton, British explorer

---

16 February 1959

Which Wimbledon tennis champion married Tatum O'Neill?

17 February 1909

Geronimo was a member of which Native American tribe?

17 February 1922

What was significant about the Irish stamp issued on this date?

18 February 1517

Which midland town was once named Maryborough?

18 February 1546

Name the German priest who led the Reformation.

18 February 1564

Which great Renaissance artist and sculptor designed the dome of St Peter's Basilica,Rome and lived to the age of 89?

18 February 1930

Which planet was discovered by Clyde Tombaugh?

18 February 1932

Amadeus, a film directed by Milos Forman, was about the lives of Antonio Salieri and which famous composer?

18 February 1933

Name John Lennon and Yoko Ono's son.

18 February 1954

John Travolta is famous for his dancing part in the film *Saturday Night Fever*. Which group made the sound track?

Birthdays	
18 February 1932	Milos Forman, Czech-American film director
18 February 1933	Yoko Ono, singer, John Lennon's widow
18 February 1954	John Travolta, American dancer and actor

19 February 1473

What nationality was Mikolaj Kopernik (Nicholas Copernicus)?

19 February 1906

Who founded the Battle Creek Toasted Corn Company, makers of breakfast cereals?

19 February 1924

Which one of these films does not feature Lee Marvin: *Gorky Park, Paint Your Wagon, The Terminator*?

19 February 1960

Name Queen Elizabeth II's two children who are older than Prince Andrew.

19 February 1982

Which Irish-based motor company went into liquidation on this date?

Birthdays	
19 February 1473	Mikolaj Kopernik (Nicholas Copernicus), Polish astronomer
19 February 1924	Lee Marvin, American actor
19 February 1960	Holly Johnson, singer (with Frankie Goes to Hollywood)

20 February 1694

Which French philosopher said, "If God did not exist, it would be necessary to invent him"?

20 February 1927

What was significant about Sidney Poitier winning an Oscar as Best Actor for his role in the film *Lilies of the Field*?

20 February 1962

Who was the first American to orbit the Earth?

Birthdays	
20 February 1925	Robert Altman, American film director (*M.A.S.H.* and *Nashville*)
21 February 1794	Antonio López de Santa Anna, President of Mexico

21 February 1794

Sam Houston defeated which Mexican leader at San Jacinto in April 1836?

21 February 1801
Which English Catholic cardinal founded University College, Dublin?

21 February 1965
Of what religion was the Black American Malcolm X, who was assassinated in 1965?

21 February 1986
Shigechiyo Izumi died in Japan on this date. Was he 105, 112, or 120?

22 February 1512
America is named after which Italian explorer?

22 February 1732
Who led the American army during the American War of Independence?

22 February 1932
Name John F. Kennedy's youngest brother.

23 February 1821
Who wrote *Ode on a Grecian Urn* and *Ode to a Nightingale*?

24 February 1841
Submarine maker John Philip Holland was born in which Co. Clare town?

24 February 1981
Which English royal engagement was announced on this date?

25 February 1936
Adolf Hitler launched the "people's car", the Volkswagen, on this date. Who designed it?

25 February 1958

The CND was founded by Bertrand Russell and others. What do the initials stand for?

25 February 1964

Sonny Liston lost his world heavyweight boxing title to Cassius Clay in 1964. What did Cassius Clay later change his name to?

Birthdays

25 February 1943   George Harrison, Beatles guitarist
26 February 1802   Victor Hugo, French writer
26 February 1932   Johnny Cash, American singer

---

26 February 1815

On which island was Napoleon originally exiled?

26 February 1839

Which sporting event was first held at Aintree, near Liverpool, on this date?

26 February 1991

Which ruler ordered a retreat and declared a victory on the same day?

27 February 1902

Tortilla Flat was the first successful novel of which famous American writer?

27 February 1932

Elizabeth Taylor has been married eight times. Who did she marry twice?

28 February 1909

Name either one of the two Nobel Prizes won by Linus Pauling.

28 February 1986
Olof Palme, who was assassinated on this date, was prime minister of which country?

29 February
What is a bissextile year?

29 February 1743
Who designed the Four Courts and the Casino at Marino?

29 February 1960
In which country is Agadir, which was destroyed by an earthquake?

MARCH

1 March 1810
What nationality was the composer Frédéric Chopin?

1 March 1886
Which wartime bandleader is best remembered for "In the Mood"?

1 March 1910
Which actor (star of *Around the World In Eighty Days*) wrote two books of memoirs, *The Moon is a Balloon* and *Bring On the Empty Horses*?

1 March 1932
The kidnapping of which aviator's baby made world headlines in 1932?

1 March 1940
Vivien Leigh won an Oscar as Best Actress for her role in which film?

1 March 1965

Which patriot had a state funeral and was buried in Glasnevin cemetery, Dublin, forty-nine years after he died?

2 March 1793

Which American statesman born in Virginia and one-time Governor of Tennessee is best remembered for defeating the Mexicans near Houston in Texas?

2 March 1969

Which supersonic aircraft had its first flight on this date?

3 March 1847

In which country was Alexander Graham Bell born?

3 March 1853

Which famous Dutch artist painted several pictures of sunflowers and irises?

3 March 1923

Which American news magazine was launched by Henry R. Luce: *Time* or *Newsweek*?

3 March 1961

Fatima Whitbread is successful at which sport?

3 March 1977

Which former Northern prime minister died after a riding accident: Terence O'Neill or Brian Faulkner?

3 March 1991

Which Englishwoman needed three stitches after being bitten by a corgi?

4 March 1678

Which composer is best remembered for *The Four Seasons*?

4 March 1975

Which silent film star received a knighthood in 1975?

Birthdays

4 March 1951	Kenny Dagleish, English soccer player and manager
5 March 1852	Lady Gregory, co-founder of the Abbey Theatre
5 March 1905	Rex Harrison, British actor
5 March 1952	Elaine Paige, British singer

---

5 March 1953

Who took charge of the Soviet Union from Lenin's death in 1924 until his own death in 1953?

5 March 1966

Dublin lost which famous landmark on this date?

6 March 1475

Who painted the ceiling of the Sistine Chapel?

6 March 1836

Where in Texas were Jim Bowie, Davy Crockett and about 150 others killed by Mexican troops?

6 March 1911

Which American actor and politician, born on this date, married Nancy Davis?

6 March 1944

The soprano Kiri Te Kanawa is a native of which country?

6 March 1987

Where did the *Herald of Free Enterprise* capsize, drowning about 200 people?

6 March 1988

Where were IRA members Seán Savage, Mairéad Farrell and Daniel McCann shot by the British SAS?

7 March 1876

What important communications device was patented by a Scottish inventor on this date?

7 March 1960

How many times has Ivan Lendl won the Wimbledon men's singles tennis title?

8 March 1917

Which German count and aviator died on this date?

9 March 1796

Which dictator married Josephine de Beauharnais on this date?

Birthdays	
9 March 1454	Amerigo Vespucci, Italian explorer
9 March 1934	Yuri Gagarin, Soviet cosmonaut

10 March 1966

Michael O'Donovan is the real name of which famous Irish short story writer?

Birthdays	
10 March 1964	Prince Edward, youngest child of Queen Elizabeth II and Prince Philip
11 March 1857	Thomas J. Clarke, 1916 leader

11 March 1931

Rupert Murdoch, newspaper proprietor, is a native of which country in the Southern Hemisphere?

11 March 1952

Douglas Adams is the humorous science-fiction writer who published a "trilogy in four parts". Name the first book in this series.

11 March 1955

Florey and Chain shared the Nobel Prize with Alexander Fleming for their work on which substance?

11 March 1985

In 1985, who became ruler of the Soviet Union after the death of Konstantin Chernenko?

12 March 1890

What kind of artiste was Vaslav Nijinsky?

12 March 1945

During the Second World War, in which Dutch city did Anne Frank and her Jewish family hide from the Nazis?

12 March 1946

Who was American singer Liza Minelli's mother?

13 March 1781

Which planet was discovered by Herschel on this date?

13 March 1960

The oldest member of the rock band U2 was born on this date. Who is he?

14 March 1879

In which country was Albert Einstein born?

14 March 1883

Who wrote *Das Kapital*?

14 March 1933

Which Cockney actor played the role of an English con-man in the film *Dirty Rotten Scoundrels*?

14 March 1991

Which miscarriage of justice was relentlessly pursued by British Labour MP Chris Mullin?

15 March 44 BC

Who was assassinated on the Ides of March?

16 March 1920

Name the old barrister played by Leo McKern in a popular British television series.

16 March 1926

What kind of craft was first launched by Robert Goddard on this date?

16 March 1940

What nationality is film director Bernardo Bertolucci?

16 March 1978

The "Red Brigades" terrorist group kidnapped and killed Aldo Moro in which European country?

17 March 1777

Patrick Prunty was born in Ireland but moved to England. He changed his name and had children named Charlotte, Emily, Anne, and Branwell. What did he change his name to?

17 March 1917

Name the Russian Tsar who was forced to give up his throne.

19 March 1906

In which country was Adolf Eichmann, the Nazi war criminal, hanged?

19 March 1932

Which famous Australian bridge was opened on this date?

19 March 1936

Ursula Andress appeared in the first James Bond film. Was that *Goldfinger, Doctor No,* or *Thunderball*?

19 March 1950

The creator of Tarzan died on this date. Who was he?

20 March 1727

Which great British scientist, once supposedly inspired by the falling of an apple, likened his achievements to examining a single pebble on the seashore?

20 March 1964

It could be said that drink killed this great Dublin writer. Who was he?

20 March 1969
Who did John Lennon marry on this date?

21 March 1685
What do J. S. Bach's initials stand for?

21 March 1963
Which American prison, now a tourist attraction, is on an island in San Francisco bay?

22 March 1903
Which great American waterfall once ran out of water because of drought?

22 March 1913
Karl Malden starred with Michael Douglas in which American television detective series?

22 March 1923
Name the French mime artist who was the only person to speak in Mel Brooks's film *Silent Movie*?

22 March 1933
One of Hitler's concentration camps was just outside Munich. Was it Auschwitz, Belsen, or Dachau?

23 March 1981
Which famous train robber was kidnapped in Brazil and brought to Barbados?

23 March 1983
What was unique about the heart Barney Clark received in a heart transplant in the United States?

24 March 1603

Which of King Henry VIII's wives was the mother of Queen Elizabeth I?

24 March 1905

Which French novelist wrote accounts of voyages to the moon and of undersea travel?

24 March 1909

Which Irish playwright wrote *Riders to the Sea*, based on stories he heard while living on the Aran Islands?

24 March 1930

Which American film star is remembered for his roles in *The Magnificent Seven* and *Bullitt*?

24 March 1953

Queen Mary, who died on this date, was the widow of which King George of England?

24 March 1976

Which German leader was beaten by Field-Marshal Montgomery at al-Alamein, Egypt?

24 March 1980

Archbishop Oscar Romero was shot dead while saying Mass in which Central American country?

24 March 1989

Off the coast of which American state did the oil tanker *Exxon Valdez* run aground?

24 March 1991

Madonna won an Oscar for her song "Sooner or Later". In which film did she sing it?

25 March 1738

Harper and composer Toirealach Ó Cearalláin was afflicted with which handicap?

25 March 1908

In which Irish county was David Lean's film *Ryan's Daughter* mainly filmed?

25 March 1914

Which famous actor, who later played the title role in *The Godfather*, played a leading role in Tennessee Williams's *A Streetcar Named Desire*?

25 March 1947

Reginald Kenneth Dwight, who had hits with "Rocket Man" and "Goodbye, Yellowbrick Road", is better known by what name?

25 March 1957

In which European city was the original EEC treaty signed?

Birthdays	
25 March 1914	Tennessee Williams, American dramatist
25 March 1942	Aretha Franklin, American soul singer
25 March 1947	Elton John, British singer
26 March 1874	Robert Frost, American poet

26 March 1827

How many symphonies did Beethoven complete during his lifetime?

26 March 1920

Which dreaded British force arrived in Ireland on this date?

26 March 1931

Leonard Nimoy played the role of which character in the original "Star Trek" television series?

26 March 1944

Name the group of singers with which Diana Ross originally found fame.

26 March 1979

Who was President of the United States when Egypt's Anwar al-Sadat and Israel's Menachem Begin signed a peace treaty?

27 March 1794

Wexfordman John Barry founded which branch of the American armed forces?

27 March 1863

Which partner designed the cars, Henry Royce or Charles Rolls?

27 March 1968

Which pioneering Soviet cosmonaut was killed in a plane crash?

27 March 1977

Where did two Boeing 747 Jumbo jets collide, killing 570 people?

28 March 1957

Jack the painter had a brother William, a writer. What is the surname of these two men?

28 March 1969

The commander-in-chief of the Allied forces during the Second World War was elected President of the United States in 1959. Who was he?

28 March 1979

What kind of leak put the Three Mile Island power plant in the news on this date?

29 March 1867

"Seward's Folly" was a name given to a wilderness purchased by the American Secretary of State William Seward from Russia. What is its real name?

29 March 1886

On this date in Atlanta, Georgia, what product did Dr John Pemberton sell for the first time?

29 March 1919

Which theory of Albert Einstein's was confirmed by experiment during a solar eclipse?

30 March 1853

In which country was Vincent van Gogh born?

30 March 1945

What was the name of Eric Clapton's son who was killed in a fall in New York in 1991?

30 March 1981

Who did John Hinckley shoot outside the Hilton Hotel in Washington?

31 March 1596
"I think, therefore I am" is a famous statement by René Descartes. He was a native of which country?

31 March 1855
Which of the Brontë sisters wrote *Jane Eyre*?

31 March 1889
Which steel structure was opened in Paris on this date?

31 March 1935
Richard Chamberlain made his name playing the title role in the "Dr Kildare" television series. Name the series in which he played the part of an English lord stranded in Japan.

31 March 1980
Where were the Olympic Games held when Jesse Owens won his four gold medals?

APRIL

1 April 1578
Name the English doctor who discovered the circulation of the blood.

1 April 1815
Otto von Bismarck was responsible for the unification of which European country?

1 April 1939
Which civil war ended on this date?

1 April 1984
Which soul singer was killed by his father, just one day before his 45th birthday?

Birthdays	
1 April 1873	Sergei Rachmaninov, Russian composer and pianist
1 April 1938	Ali McGraw, American actress
1 April 1939	Rudolf Isley, American pop singer

2 April 1805
Name the Danish shoemaker's son who went on to become one of the world's great storytellers.

2 April 1865
At the end of the American Civil War, which general (and future president) accepted General Robert E. Lee's surrender?

2 April 1982
Name the two countries involved in the Falklands War.

3 April 1783

Which character, created by Washington Irving, fell asleep in the Catskill Mountains?

3 April 1860

Which delivery service took mail from St Joseph's, Missouri, to Sacramento, California?

3 April 1882

Which of the James brothers, Jesse or Frank, was killed by one of their own gang members?

3 April 1924

Which actor played the title role in the film *The Godfather*?

3 April 1930

Name the Chancellor (Prime Minister) of Germany who presided over the reunification of his country.

3 April 1936

Bruno Hauptmann, who was executed for kidnapping and killing Charles Lindbergh's baby, was an illegal immigrant from which European country?

3 April 1961

Name the actor who played the title role in *Beverly Hills Cop*.

3 April 1991

He wrote *The Power and the Glory*, *The Comedians*, and *Our Man In Havana*, and he died on this date. Who was he?

4 April 1949
Which military treaty was signed by Belgium, Britain, Canada, Denmark, France, Iceland, Italy, Luxembourg, the Netherlands, Norway, Portugal, and the United States?

4 April 1968
In which American state is Memphis, scene of the assassination of civil rights leader Martin Luther King?

4 April 1981 (a)
What disease did Bob Champion overcome before he won the Grand National?

4 April 1981 (b)
In which city did Bucks Fizz win the Eurovision Song Contest with "Making Your Mind Up"?

5 April 1964
Is the American general Douglas MacArthur remembered for liberating the Philippines or for liberating Normandy?

Birthdays	
5 April 1725	Giovanni Casanova, Italian adventurer
5 April 1900	Spencer Tracy, American actor
5 April 1908	Herbert von Karajan, German conductor
5 April 1908	Bette Davis, American actress
5 April 1916	Gregory Peck, American actor
6 April 1929	André Previn, German-American conductor

6 April 1874
What was the stage name of Ehrich Weiss, a famous Hungarian-American escape artist?

6 April 1896

Which sporting event opened in Athens on this date and has been held every four years (apart from war years) ever since?

6 April 1909

What nationality was Robert Peary, the first person to reach the North Pole?

6 April 1917

Which large country entered the First World War nearly three years after it began?

6 April 1926

Which clergyman founded the Democratic Unionist Party?

7 April 1739

Name the butcher-turned-highwayman who was hanged on this date.

7 April 1891

Name the children's building blocks that were invented by Ole Kirk Christiansen.

7 April 1947

Who made cars and offered them in any colour provided it was black?

7 April 1968

Jim Clark was killed at Hockenheim, Germany. What sport was he taking part in at the time?

7 April 1973

Archbishop John Charles McQuaid was the bishop of which Irish diocese?

8 April 1893

Mary Pickford made a name for herself in which profession?

8 April 1963

Julian is the first name of the son of which member of the Beatles?

8 April 1973

Picasso was a Spaniard, but in which country did he spend most of his life?

8 April 1986

Who did the people of Carmel, California, elect as their mayor on this date?

9 April 1959

Name a famous American architect who had the same surname as a pair of famous aviators.

9 April 1961

There really was a King Zog, and he died on this date. Of which European country was he king?

9 April 1981

Name the republican hunger-striker who won a seat in the British Parliament.

Birthdays
9 April 1806   Isambard Kingdom Brunel,
                      British engineer and shipbuilder

---

10 April 1989

Which English golfer, legendary for his performances at the Carroll's Irish Open, was the first European to win the US Masters golf tournament?

11 April 1929
A certain spinach-eating cartoon character was "born" on this date. Who was he?

12 April 1861
Which side fired the first shot in the American Civil War: the Union or Confederate side?

12 April 1928 (a)
Which Irish newspaper was the first European newspaper to cross the Atlantic?

12 April 1928 (b)
What was significant about Col. James Fitzmaurice's flight across the Atlantic in a plane named *Bremen*?

12 April 1941
Bobby Moore was the captain of the English soccer team that won the World Cup—in which year?

12 April 1945
President Franklin D. Roosevelt died in office on this date. Who was the next President of the United States to die in office?

12 April 1954
Which early rock and roll hit was recorded by Bill Haley and the Comets in 1954?

12 April 1961
Name the first human being in space.

12 April 1981 (a)
What space achievement was made by the United States exactly twenty years after the world saw the first person in space?

12 April 1981 (b)
Which American boxer had the nickname "the Brown Bomber"?

13 April 1742
In which city was Handel's *Messiah* first performed?

13 April 1743
The heads of four American presidents are carved on the side of Mount Rushmore: George Washington, Thomas Jefferson, Abraham Lincoln, and Theodore Roosevelt. Which of them was born on this date?

13 April 1829
From an Irish point of view, which important Act of the British Parliament came into force on this date?

13 April 1906
Which Irish writer wrote *Endgame* and *Waiting for Godot*?

13 April 1980
When golfer Seve Ballesteros won the US Open at Augusta, Georgia, on this date, he was the first European to do so and also the youngest to do so. Was he 23, 24, or 25?

14 April 1527
What was the name once given to Daingean, Co. Offaly?

14 April 1865
Where was Abraham Lincoln assassinated?

14 April 1912

Which iceberg made history forty-nine years after the assassination of Abraham Lincoln?

15 April 1955

Which chain of restaurants opened its first premises in San Bernardino, California?

15 April 1986

Name the Libyan city that was bombed on the orders of Ronald Reagan.

15 April 1989

In which English city is Hillsboro Stadium, scene of the disaster in which ninety-five soccer fans were crushed to death?

16 April 1850

Name the French woman who founded a famous waxworks in London.

16 April 1867

Which was the older brother, Orville or Wilbur Wright?

16 April 1889

When he starred in *The Great Dictator* in 1940, which European ruler was Charlie Chaplin ridiculing?

Birthdays

16 April 1889	Charlie Chaplin, English comedian
16 April 1924	Henry Mancini, American composer
17 April 1929	James Last, German bandleader

---

17 April 1790

Which American scientist, who invented the lightning conductor, was once America's ambassador in Paris?

17 April 1970

Which crippled Apollo space mission had to use the power of their moon-landing module to get them home?

18 April 1775

Which American patriot rode from Charleston to Lexington to warn his comrades that British soldiers were approaching?

18 April 1906

Which American west coast city was devastated by an earthquake on this date?

19 April 1882

Which nineteenth-century scientist shocked society by suggesting that humans were descended from apes?

19 April 1956

She was the first film star to have her portrait on a postage stamp, after she married a European prince. Who was she?

19 April 1993

Where in Texas did David Koresh and over ninety members of his Branch Davidian religious cult commit mass suicide?

20 April 1889

Which soldier, who was promoted to corporal during the First World War, went on to become the ruler of Germany?

20 April 1912

Name the Irishman who created Dracula.

20 April 1941

Tennis player John McEnroe married Tatum, the daughter of which American film star?

20 April 1955

Name either of the two European countries where Albert Einstein lived before moving to America.

21 April 1816
Which of the Brontë sisters used the pen name Currer Bell?

21 April 1910
The writer of *Huckleberry Finn* was correct when he predicted that he would die in the year that Halley's Comet returned. Who was he?

21 April 1918
By what name was First World War veteran Manfred von Richtofen also known?

22 April 1870
The Russian city of St Petersburg used to be named after which communist leader?

22 April 1904
During the Second World War, scientist Robert Oppenheimer was in charge of which secret project?

22 April 1926
Queen Elizabeth II has one sister. Name her.

22 April 1933
Who died first, Mr Rolls or Mr Royce?

23 April 1616
Apart from being writers, what have England's William Shakespeare and Spain's Miguel de Cervantes got in common?

Birthdays
23 April 1775   William Turner, English artist
23 April 1936   Roy Orbison, blind American singer

---

24 April 1731

Who wrote *Robinson Crusoe*?

24 April 1916

Which of the Easter Rising leaders founded St Enda's School?

24 April 1934

What is the name of Shirley MacLaine's brother who starred in *Bugsy, Bonnie and Clyde,* and *Heaven Can Wait*?

24 April 1981

What did Brazilian resident Ronald Biggs rob in England in 1963?

24 April 1986

Wallis Simpson was the widow of which member of the British royal family?

Birthdays

24 April 1815	Anthony Trollope, English writer
24 April 1916	William Joyce ("Lord Haw-Haw"), Irish-American broadcaster who worked for Germany during the Second World War

---

25 April 1599

Name the man who killed thousands of Irish people and was Lord Protector of England after the death of King Charles I.

25 April 1719

Which novel, set on a desert island, was first published on this date?

25 April 1874

His mother was a Jameson, a member of the whiskey-distilling family, and his father was Italian. He won the Nobel Prize for Physics. Who was he?

25 April 1939

Has Al Pacino, star of the three "Godfather" films, ever won an Oscar?

25 April 1990

What is the name of the telescope that was launched into orbit on this date?

26 April 1452

The Last Supper is painted on the wall of a monastery refectory in Italy. *Mona Lisa* is hanging in the Louvre. Who painted these masterpieces?

26 April 1894

During which war did Rudolf Hess fly to Britain seeking to make a settlement?

26 April 1937

The Basque town of Gernika (Guernica) was bombed by German planes supporting Gen. Francisco Franco. During what war did this event happen?

26 April 1986

Is Chernobyl in Belarus (Byelorussia) or Ukraine?

26 April 1989

"I Love Lucy" is a popular television comedy series. What was the full name of the red-haired Lucy?

27 April 1521
Name the group of islands in Asia where the famous Portuguese navigator Fernão de Magalhães (Ferdinand Magellan) was killed.

27 April 1791
Who invented the code that uses a series of dots and dashes to send a message?

27 April 1827
In which country did Ulysses S. Grant prove to be a brilliant general but a terrible president?

27 April 1937
Name the bridge that links Marin County to the city of San Francisco.

27 April 1953
Maud Gonne MacBride was the mother of diplomat Seán MacBride. In her time she was loved by a famous writer. Who was he?

28 April 1770
Which modern Australian city lies close to Botany Bay?

28 April 1789 (a)
Fletcher Christian was the leader of which famous mutiny in the South Pacific?

28 April 1789 (b)
Who was the captain of that ship?

28 April 1945
Name the European dictator killed by his own fellow-citizens close to the end of the Second World War.

28 April 1980
Which British-American film director noted for his suspense films, including *The Birds* and *Psycho*, died on this date?

29 April 1769
Which famous person born in Ireland is supposed to have said, "Not everything born in a stable is a horse," when asked if he was an Irishman?

29 April 1889
Why was jazz musician Edward Ellington nicknamed "Duke"?

29 April 1938
Former European Commissioner Ray MacSharry had responsibility for which department: Competition, Agriculture, or Social Affairs?

29 April 1945
Who did Eva Braun marry the day before she died?

30 April 1789
In which city was George Washington sworn in as the first President of the United States: Washington, New York, or Philadelphia?

30 April 1945
Who left orders for his body to be burned after he committed suicide?

MAY

1 May 1854
Which songwriter wrote "Are Ye Right There, Michael?" and "Phil The Fluther's Ball"?

1 May 1931

Name the building, the world's highest at the time, that was opened by President Herbert Hoover of the United States.

1 May 1945

As well as killing himself, which Nazi leader killed his wife and six children: Goebbels, Eichmann, or Hess?

1 May 1960

Which pop singer was born ten days after American Gary Powers's spy plane was shot down over the Soviet Union?

1 May 1967

Priscilla Beaulieu is now a widow and uses her late husband's name. Which famous music star did she marry?

1 May 1968

A tourist attraction known as Legoland is in which European country?

2 May 1519

Which famous Renaissance artist and scientist wrote his notes in mirror writing?

2 May 1856

Which holy man from Dublin's inner city was born on this date?

2 May 1892

Which famous German fighter pilot had his birthday on this date?

2 May 1904

Which song, written by Irving Berlin and recorded by Bing Crosby, was the biggest-selling record of all time?

2 May 1923

Who was President of Ireland immediately before Mary Robinson?

2 May 1969

Name the British ocean liner that had its inaugural voyage on this date.

2 May 1972

Which powerful American detective agency was headed by J. Edgar Hoover from 1924 until his death on this date?

2 May 1982

The cruiser *General Belgrano* was sunk by the British nuclear submarine *Conqueror* on this date. To which country did the *General Belgrano* belong?

3 May 1916

Which one of the 1916 Rising leaders was designated President of the Provisional Government?

4 May 1852

Which famous children's writer modelled his fictitious character on a real girl called Alice Liddell?

4 May 1873

Which nineteenth-century explorer died in Old Chitambo, Zambia, and was buried at Westminster Abbey, London?

4 May 1929

Which Belgian-American actress starred with Rex Harrison in *My Fair Lady*?

4 May 1979

Name the woman who replaced James Callaghan as Prime Minister of Britain.

4 May 1980

Under President Tito, Croatia, Bosnia, Serbia and other nations were united as one country. Name the country.

5 May 1821

Where did Napoleon die?

5 May 1943

Michael Palin, John Cleese, Graham Chapman and Eric Idle were all members of which famous comedy team?

5 May 1961

Who was the first American in space: John Glenn, Alan Shepard, or Neil Armstrong?

5 May 1981

Republican prisoner Bobby Sands died after sixty-six days on hunger-strike. In which month did he begin his fast?

6 May 1626

Europeans of which nationality paid trinkets to Native Americans for Manhattan Island?

6 May 1840

What was the Penny Black?

6 May 1856

Psychoanalyst Sigmund Freud was born in Freiburg and spent most of his life in Vienna. In which country did he die?

6 May 1882

In which Dublin park were Chief Secretary Cavendish and Under-Secretary Burke brutally murdered?

6 May 1895

Rudolf Valentino, a star in early romantic silent films, was born in which country?

6 May 1910

King Edward VII, who reigned for nine years, was the son of which British monarch?

6 May 1915

Born in America on this date, he appeared in the Gate Theatre, Dublin, in 1931, became a star with *Citizen Kane* and other films, and died in 1985. Who was he?

6 May 1937

Modern airships are filled with the safe gas helium. Name the hydrogen-filled airship that exploded at Lakehurst, New Jersey, on this date.

6 May 1954

In which British university city did Roger Bannister run the first four-minute mile on this date?

6 May 1983

The proprietors of *Stern*, a German news magazine, found that they had paid a fortune for a collection of diaries that were forgeries. Which famous person was supposed to have written them?

7 May 1823

Which of Beethoven's symphonies is known as the Choral Symphony?

7 May 1840

Who composed the music for the ballets *Swan Lake* and *The Sleeping Beauty*?

7 May 1901

Which classic western film starred Gary Cooper and Grace Kelly?

7 May 1915

Irish art collector Sir Hugh Lane drowned when the ship he was travelling on was torpedoed by a German submarine. Name the ship.

7 May 1936

Which former Irish international rugby player is involved with Independent Newspapers and the Heinz food company?

7 May 1945

At the end of the Second World War, who surrendered first, the Germans or the Japanese?

8 May 1828

Which international relief organisation was founded by Swiss citizen Henri Dunant?

8 May 1884

The man who became President of the United States on the death of Franklin Roosevelt had a sign on his desk saying *The buck stops here.* Who was he?

8 May 1902

Two people survived when the volcano Mount Pelee erupted on the island of Martinique. In which sea is Martinique?

8 May 1940

Which book by Peter Benchley was turned into Steven Spielberg's first blockbuster film?

8 May 1945

In Britain on this date, why did everybody get a day off?

9 May 1926

Which American explorer flew over the North Pole on this date and over the South Pole in 1929?

9 May 1860

The royalties of which work by J. M. Barrie belong to a London children's hospital?

10 May 1838

John Wilkes Booth assassinated which American president?

10 May 1863

Gen. Thomas "Stonewall" Jackson died from gunshot wounds fired by a soldier on his own side during the American Civil War. Which side was Jackson on: Union or Confederate?

10 May 1869

What kind of transport vehicles met at Promontory Point, Utah, on this date?

10 May 1899

Film stars Fred Astaire and Ginger Rogers are particularly remembered for which performing talent?

10 May 1904

The man who said, "Dr Livingstone, I presume?" died on this date. Who was he?

10 May 1940

Who took over as Prime Minister of Britain about eight months after the beginning of the Second World War?

10 May 1960

What is Bono's real name?

11 May 1904

Unlike Picasso, Salvador Dali spent most of his life in his home country. Name the homeland of both Picasso and Dali.

11 May 1971

He resigned as Taoiseach in 1966 and died on this date. Who was he?

11 May 1981

Bob Marley, who died of cancer aged 36, was famous for what kind of music?

11 May 1985

An English football stadium burst into flames, killing forty people. In which city did this tragedy happen?

11 May 1988

Why was this date a good one for Irving Berlin to celebrate?

12 May 1820

Which dedicated nurse helped the wounded during the Crimean War?

12 May 1932
German immigrant Bruno Hauptmann kidnapped and killed the baby of which well-known American pilot?

13 May 1842
Who wrote the music for the Gilbert and Sullivan operas: Gilbert or Sullivan?

13 May 1954
This is the birthday of which successful Eurovision Song Contest entrant?

13 May 1981
Which leader survived being shot by Mehmet Ali Agca?

Birthdays	
13 May 1914	Joe Louis, American boxer
14 May 1727	Thomas Gainsborough, English painter

14 May 1948
Of which state, founded on this date, was David Ben-Gurion first Prime Minister?

15 May 1847
His heart is in Rome; the rest of his body is in Glasnevin; and his portrait is on the £20 note. Who was this prominent nineteenth-century Irish politician?

15 May 1953
Who wrote the instrumental musical piece "Tubular Bells"?

15 May 1993 (a)
Where did Niamh Kavanagh win the Eurovision Song Contest?

15 May 1993 (b)
Name the song she sang.

16 May 1905
Father of Jane and Peter, this famous film star was born in Nebraska. Who was he?

16 May 1919
Liberace will be remembered as an extravagant showman. What instrument did he play?

16 May 1955
Did Russian gymnast Olga Korbut win her Olympic gold medals at Munich or Montréal?

17 May 1900
Which Islamic republic was ruled by the Ayatollah Khomeini?

17 May 1969
What kind of power did Dubliner Tom McLean use on the small boat he took from Newfoundland to Blacksod Bay, Co. Mayo?

18 May 1804
Who crowned Napoleon Emperor of France?

18 May 1868
Tsar Nikolai (Nicholas) II married the granddaughter of which British monarch?

18 May 1919
In the later half of her career, who was Margot Fonteyn's famous dancing partner?

18 May 1920
By what name is Karol Wojtyla better known?

18 May 1980
Which volcano erupted in Oregon on this date?

19 May 1536
Which of King Henry VIII's wives was beheaded first?

19 May 1926
Which Black American Muslim leader, assassinated in 1965, was the subject of a film released in 1992?

19 May 1935
In a film directed by David Lean, Peter O'Toole played the part of which First World War hero?

20 May 1506
Which explorer was first buried in Spain, then in Hispaniola, then in Spain again?

20 May 1932
Who was the first woman to fly solo across the Atlantic Ocean?

Birthdays	
20 May 1945	Cher, American singer and actress
21 May 1471	Albrecht Dürer, German artist
21 May 1608	Alexander Pope, English poet
21 May 1921	Andrei Sakharov, Russian physicist and Nobel Peace Prize winner
21 May 1944	Mary Robinson, President of Ireland

21 May 1927
When Charles Lindbergh made the first solo Atlantic crossing, in which European capital city did he land?

21 May 1944
What was President Mary Robinson's maiden name?

21 May 1991
While touring India during an election campaign, which son of Indira Gandhi was assassinated?

22 May 1859
Who created Sherlock Holmes?

22 May 1885
Who wrote the novel on which the musical *Les Misérables* is based?

22 May 1907
Which famous English actor won an Oscar for his roles as King Henry IV and Hamlet?

22 May 1932
Lady Gregory was one of the co-founders of which Dublin theatre?

22 May 1946
Which former Manchester United player, born on this date, opened the Manchester United shop in Belfast in 1993?

22 May 1981
Who was sentenced to life imprisonment for the murder of several women in and around Yorkshire?

23 May 1498
Vasco da Gama was the first European to reach which Asian country by sea?

23 May 1701
How did Captain Kidd make a living?

23 May 1933
Joan is an actress and Jackie is a novelist. What is the surname of these two talented sisters?

23 May 1934
Which American gangster duo were gunned down on this date?

23 May 1945
Heinrich Himmler committed suicide to avoid going on trial for war crimes. In which German city were the trials of Nazi war criminals taking place?

24 May 1809
Which prison on the Devon moors was originally opened for French prisoners of war?

24 May 1819
Queen Victoria was born on this date. In which year did she die?

24 May 1844
Who was the first person to send a Morse code message?

24 May 1883
Which landmark, linking the Brooklyn and Manhattan areas of New York, was opened on this date?

24 May 1928
In which Co. Cork town was short-story writer William Trevor born?

24 May 1941
Robert Zimmermann, the writer of "Mr Tambourine Man" and other songs, is better known by what name?

25 May 1916
Which famous car manufacturer said, "History is bunk"?

25 May 1986

The Sport-Aid Race Against Time, in which 30 million people ran, raised money to help the poor of which continent?

26 May 1886

Name the first talking film, in which Al Jolson played the title role.

26 May 1907

Marion Morrison was the original name of which actor famous for his tough-guy films?

26 May 1988

Which musical, based on some poems by T. S. Eliot, opened in Moscow on this date?

27 May 1703

Name the Russian city built by Tsar Pyotr I (Peter the Great) as his capital city.

27 May 1940

During the Second World War, which beach was evacuated with the aid of thousands of British citizens who crossed the English Channel in their own boats?

Birthdays	
27 May 1837	James "Wild Bill" Hickok, American lawman
27 May 1878	Isadora Duncan, American dancer
27 May 1911	Vincent Price, British star of horror films
27 May 1923	Henry Kissinger, German-American diplomat

28 May 1968

Which "Neighbours" actress became a successful pop singer?

28 May 1972

Which British king was given the title Duke of Windsor after he gave up his throne to marry Mrs Simpson?

28 May 1987

Where in the Soviet Union did 19-year-old Mattias Rust land his small plane?

28 May 1990

In which European country is Roermond, where the IRA shot dead two Australian tourists on this date?

Birthdays	
28 May 1738	Joseph Guillotin, French doctor who invented the guillotine
28 May 1779	Thomas Moore, Irish poet
28 May 1908	Ian Fleming, creator of James Bond

29 May 1453

Which city, located where Europe meets Asia, was taken by the Turks?

29 May 1911

Which half of the Gilbert and Sullivan team died in a drowning accident?

29 May 1914

On which river on the US-Canadian border did the *Empress of Ireland* sink, killing about a thousand people?

29 May 1953
On John F. Kennedy's 36th birthday, who climbed Mount Everest?

29 May 1985
Where is the Heysel Stadium, where forty-one people were killed at a European Cup Final soccer match between Liverpool and Juventus?

Birthdays	
29 May 1874	G. K. Chesterton, British writer
29 May 1903	Bob Hope, British-American comedian
29 May 1917	John F. Kennedy, American president

30 May 1536
Who did King Henry VIII marry shortly after the death of Anne Boleyn?

30 May 1911
Which famous motor race is held in Indiana on Memorial Day, a US national holiday on the last Monday in May?

30 May 1912
How did flight pioneer Wilbur Wright die?

30 May 1959
Christopher Cockerell launched which new type of craft off the Isle of Wight, England?

30 May 1960
Which novel by Boris Pasternak was made into a film by David Lean?

30 May 1973
Erskine Childers was elected President of Ireland on this date. Who was the next President to be elected by the people?

Birthdays	
30 May 1846	Peter Carl Fabergé, goldsmith, best known for the Fabergé Eggs he made for the Russian royal family
30 May 1908	Mel Blanc, the voice of Bugs Bunny and Daffy Duck
30 May 1909	Benny Goodman, jazz clarinet player

31 May 1809
Franz Josef Haydn was a native of which European country?

31 May 1837
What was the profession of Englishman Joe Grimaldi?

31 May 1927
To the nearest million, how many Model T Fords were made?

31 May 1930
Who played the role of tough San Francisco policeman Dirty Harry?

31 May 1965
What was significant about Jim Clark's winning the Indianapolis 500 on this date?

Birthdays	
31 May 1965	Brooke Shields, American actress

JUNE

1 June 1762

The founder of the Christian Brothers was born near Callan, Co. Kilkenny. Who was he?

1 June 1910

Who set out from London on this date and became the leader of the second expedition to reach the South Pole?

1 June 1926

Norma Jean Baker was the original name of which famous film actress?

1 June 1967

How many albums did the Beatles release after "Sergeant Pepper's Lonely Hearts Club Band"?

1 June 1968 (a)

Anne Sullivan taught which blind and deaf person to speak?

1 June 1968 (b)

Which "Neighbours" actor went on to have a successful singing career?

1 June 1971

What is the name (beginning with Z) of the African country formerly called Rhodesia?

2 June 1740

Which English word is derived from the name of the Marquis de Sade?

2 June 1896

Who on this date patented a system for long-distance communicating without wires?

2 June 1953

In which church was Queen Elizabeth II crowned?

2 June 1954

To which post was John A. Costello elected on this date?

2 June 1987

What kind of Australian animal took the baby of Lindy Chamberlain?

2 June 1990

Who played the role of Prof. Henry Higgins in the film *My Fair Lady*?

Birthdays	
2 June 1840	Thomas Hardy, English writer
2 June 1857	Edward Elgar, English composer

3 June 1899

Was "The Blue Danube" written by Johann Strauss the Younger or Johann Strauss the Elder?

3 June 1946

Which kind of swimsuit got its name from an atomic bomb test site in the Pacific?

3 June 1963

Which pope, who died on this date, was *Time* magazine's Man of the Year for 1962?

3 June 1965

Edward H. White was the first person to walk in space. Did he perform this feat from a Mercury or Gemini spacecraft?

Birthdays	
3 June 1808	Jefferson Davis, President of the Confederate States during the American Civil War
3 June 1878	Sinéad Ní Fhlannagáin, wife of Éamon de Valera
3 June 1925	Tony Curtis, American actor and father of Jamie Lee Curtis
3 June 1950	Suzi Quattro, American rock star

4 June 1941
Which kaiser (king) ruled Germany during the First World War?

4 June 1944
Which European capital city was liberated before the Normandy invasion?

4 June 1989 (a)
In which country did over 460 people die when a gas pipe running alongside a railway line leak and explode?

4 June 1989 (b)
In which city is Tienanmen Square, where the authorities slaughtered thousands of protesting students?

5 June 1783
Name the French brothers who launched the first hot air balloon on this date.

5 June 1868
James Connolly was born in Cowgate, an area of which Scottish city?

5 June 1916

Irish-born Earl Kitchener was commander-in-chief in South Africa during which war at the turn of the century?

5 June 1920

Which book written by Irishman Cornelius Ryan outlines the events of the Normandy invasion?

5 June 1967

Egypt, Jordan and Syria fought which country during the "Six-Day War"?

6 June 1944

What were Juno, Omaha and Sword code names for?

6 June 1949

The title of which book written by George Orwell is simply a date?

6 June 1968

Which politician, running in an American presidential election, was gunned down and killed in Los Angeles?

6 June 1976

J. Paul Getty, one of the world's richest people, made his money dealing in which commodity?

Birthdays	
6 June 1799	Aleksandr Pushkin, Russian writer
6 June 1868	Capt. Robert Scott, British explorer
6 June 1956	Bjorn Borg, Swedish world tennis champion

7 June 1329

Which Scottish leader was supposed to have been inspired by watching a spider in a cave on Rathlin Island?

7 June 1905

Which Scandinavian country was ruled by Sweden until 1905?

7 June 1909

The oldest actress to win an Oscar did so for her role in *Driving Miss Daisy*. Who was she?

7 June 1982

Which star once lived at Graceland, now a tourist attraction?

Birthdays	
7 June 1848	Paul Gauguin, French artist
7 June 1892	Kevin O'Higgins, Irish politician
7 June 1909	Jessica Tandy, American actress
7 June 1958	Prince, American singer

8 June 1986

Kurt Waldheim, once Secretary-General of the United Nations, became the president of which European country?

Birthdays	
8 June 1869	Frank Lloyd Wright, American architect
8 June 1940	Nancy Sinatra, American singer, daughter of Frank
9 June 1781	George Stephenson, English railway engineer

9 June 1870

He died before completing his novel *The Mystery of Edwin Drood*, but had huge success with his earlier novels, including *Hard Times* and *A Tale of Two Cities*. Who was he?

9 June 1898
Due to be handed back in 1997, Hong Kong was leased by China to Britain for what length of time?

9 June 1934
Which famous Walt Disney character made his first appearance in *The Wise Little Hen*?

10 June 1967
Which Middle East country emerged victorious from the "Six-Day War"?

10 June 1991
Where is Mount Pinatubo, which erupted fiercely on this date?

Birthdays	
10 June 1921	Prince Philip, husband of Queen Elizabeth II
11 June 1776	John Constable, English landscape painter
11 June 1910	Jacques Cousteau, French undersea explorer
11 June 1912	Mary Lavin, Irish short-story writer
11 June 1918	Nelson Mandela, South African statesman
11 June 1935	Gene Wilder, American comic actor

11 June 1509
King Henry VIII of England married his first wife when he was 18 and she was 24. Who was she?

11 June 1955
At which French motoring event did a Mercedes car go out of control and kill eighty spectators?

12 June 1819
Who created *The Water Babies*?

12 June 1965
The MBE (Member of the Order of the British Empire) was awarded to which famous pop group on this date?

12 June 1991
In Russia's first democratic election, who was elected President?

13 June 1865
W. B. Yeats was a co-founder of which theatre?

13 June 1944
Which country used rocket-powered bombs during the Second World War?

14 June 1884
Which midland town is the birthplace of John McCormack?

14 June 1928
Revolutionary Ernesto (Che) Guevara was born in Argentina, but in which neighbouring South American country did he die?

14 June 1940
Which capital city was taken by the German army on this date?

14 June 1964
Which political activist was sentenced to prison on this date and not released until 1990?

14 June 1968
Which German won the Wimbledon tennis championships first: Steffi Graf or Boris Becker?

15 June 1215

Which document was signed by King John of England at Runnymede?

15 June 1919

Name the pilots of the plane that crash-landed in Connemara on this date.

16 June 1890

Which one of the Laurel and Hardy team was born on this date?

16 June 1904

All the events of *Ulysses*, which is set in Dublin, happen on a single day—16 June 1904. Which Irishman wrote the novel?

16 June 1961

Which ballet dancer defected from the Soviet Union while visiting Paris?

16 June 1972

A burglary-gone-wrong in the offices of the Democratic Party led to the downfall of President Richard Nixon. What is the name of the building where the burglary took place?

17 June 1977

Which American government agency employed German rocket scientist Werner von Braun?

18 June 1815

Who defeated Napolean at the Battle of Waterloo?

18 June 1928

Which Antarctic explorer was killed in a plane crash in the Arctic while searching for a fellow-explorer?

18 June 1942
Name the band formed by Paul McCartney after the Beatles split up.

19 June 1937
Who wrote *Peter Pan*?

19 June 1947
Name the book written by Salman Rushdie that moved Iran's Ayatollah Khomeini to issue his death sentence.

20 June 1763
Before the 1798 Rising, from which country did Wolfe Tone seek assistance?

20 June 1837
Which woman succeeded King William IV on the throne of England?

Birthdays
20 June 1906   Catherine Cookson, British writer
20 June 1949   Lionel Ritchie, American singer
21 June 1982   Prince William,
                        son of Charles and Diana

---

21 June 1970
At which sport did Brazil win and keep the Jules Rimet Cup?

22 June 1929
Ireland's first commemorative stamp marked the centenary of which event?

22 June 1936
Kris Kristofferson has two careers. One is as an actor; what is the other?

22 June 1949

Which talented actress has appeared with Dustin Hoffman in *Kramer v. Kramer* and with Robert Redford in *Out of Africa*?

23 June 1848

What kind of object was patented by Adolphe Sax in 1848?

23 June 1875

What did Isaac Singer invent?

23 June 1985

An Air India Boeing 747 exploded off the Irish coast, killing the 329 people on board. Where was the plane coming from?

24 June 1314

Who won the Battle of Bannockburn: the Scots or the English?

24 June 1973

Who preceded Erskine Childers as President of Ireland?

25 June 1876

Who made a mistake when counting Sioux warriors near Little Bighorn, Montana?

25 June 1964

Who did Irish broadcaster Gay Byrne marry?

Birthdays	
24 June 1850	Horatio Kitchener, Kerry-born British soldier
25 June 1900	Lord Mountbatten, British statesman and member of the royal family
25 June 1903	George Orwell, British writer
25 June 1945	Carly Simon, American singer
25 June 1963	George Michael, British singer

26 June 1963
After visiting Germany, which country did President Kennedy visit next?

26 June 1976
Viking I beamed back photographs of the surface of which planet in the Solar System?

27 June 1846
Where was Charles Stewart Parnell's home?

Birthdays	
27 June 1880	Helen Keller, American blind and deaf teacher and writer
28 June 1491	King Henry VIII of England
28 June 1926	Mel Brooks, American comedian and film director

28 June 1861
Robert O'Hara-Burke was the first person to cross which continent?

28 June 1914
The assassination of Archduke Franz Ferdinand sparked a series of events that led to the First World War. In which Bosnian city did the assassination take place?

28 June 1986
Which successful businessman and adventurer crossed the Atlantic in *Challenger II*?

29 June 1986
Which country, helped by Diego Maradonna, won the World Cup soccer championship on this date?

30 June 1894
Tower Bridge, opened by the Prince of Wales, crosses which English river?

30 June 1936
How many novels did *Gone with the Wind* writer Margaret Mitchell write?

JULY

1 July 1681
Which Irishman was the last Catholic to be martyred at Tyburn in England?

1 July 1863
During the American Civil War, which battle raged from 1 to 3 July 1863?

1 July 1916 (a)
Which well-known soft drinks bottle was launched on this date?

1 July 1916 (b)
Which First World War battle lasted over four months and claimed the lives of over 420,000 British soldiers?

1 July 1961
Jesse Owens won four gold medals at the 1936 Olympics in Berlin. Which Black American repeated the feat in Los Angeles in 1984?

2 July 1865
Name the army established by William Booth.

2 July 1900

Which German count had a success with his flying machine on this date?

2 July 1922

Which prominent Dublin quayside building was blown up on this date?

3 July 1987

When did the "Butcher of Lyons", Klaus Barbie, commit his crimes?

3 July 1988

Where did the American warship *Vincennes* make the mistake of shooting down an Iranian passenger plane, killing 286 people?

4 July 1776

The Americans declared their independence from which European country?

4 July 1826

What is notable about the date of the death of former US Presidents John Adams and Thomas Jefferson?

4 July 1881

Which 22-year-old outlaw was shot dead by Pat Garrett?

4 July 1976

Israel mounted a raid on Entebbe airport to free some of its citizens trapped after an airline hijack. In which African country is Entebbe?

5 July 1826
Which Asian city, now a city-state, was founded by Sir Thomas Stamford Raffles?

5 July 1975
Who defeated Jimmy Connors to become the first black person to win the men's singles championship at Wimbledon?

6 July 1535
The author of *Utopia* was a member of the court of King Henry VIII and was beheaded for not abandoning his Catholic beliefs. Who was he?

6 July 1946
Who was the star of the "Rocky" and "Rambo" series of films?

6 July 1971
Which jazz trumpeter died three days after his 71st birthday?

7 July 1930
Which detective featured in *The Hound of the Baskervilles*?

7 July 1982
Which royal person had her sleep disturbed by Michael Fagin, who sneaked into her bedroom?

7 July 1985
What age was Boris Becker when he won his first Wimbledon tennis title?

7 July 1990

Which woman won a record-breaking nine Wimbledon tennis championships?

Birthdays	
8 July 1838	Count Ferdinand von Zeppelin, German airship maker

8 July 1853

Which Asian country reluctantly opened itself to the influence of the outside world after Commodore Perry of the US Navy arrived on this date?

8 July 1967

Which star of the film *Gone with the Wind* died of TB at the age of 53?

8 July 1978

What was significant about Reinhold Messner and Peter Habeler climbing Mount Everest on this date?

Birthdays	
9 July 1901	Barbara Cartland, British romance writer
9 July 1916	Edward Heath, British politician and former Prime Minister
9 July 1937	David Hockney, British artist

10 July 1834

Whistler's painting *An Arrangement in Grey and Black* is better known by what name?

10 July 1927

Which controversial Irish politician was murdered while walking to Mass in Booterstown, Dublin?

10 July 1985 (a)

In which country was the Greenpeace ship *Rainbow Warrior* when it was blown up and sunk?

10 July 1985 (b)

Agents from which country were responsible for sinking *Rainbow Warrior*?

11 July 1690

Where in Ireland did King William III defeat King James II?

11 July 1915

Which bald actor is best remembered for his roles in *The King and I* and *The Magnificent Seven*?

12 July 1910

Which one of the Rolls-Royce team was the first person in Britain to be killed in a plane crash?

12 July 1937

Which Black American actor starred in his own successful television situation comedy series?

12 July 1949

Which former President of Ireland wrote folk-tales under the pen name An Craoibhín Aoibhinn?

13 July 1942

What is the name of the first "Indiana Jones" film starring Harrison Ford?

14 July 1789

Who was President of France during the celebrations marking the 200th anniversary of the French Revolution?

15 July

This date is the feast day of which saint and alleged weather forecaster?

15 July 1606

The Dutch painter of *The Night Watch* left a large legacy of self-portraits. Who was he?

15 July 1899

Who was Taoiseach during John F. Kennedy's visit to Ireland?

15 July 1904

Which Russian writer is equally famous for his plays and his short stories?

15 July 1927

Which Irishwoman was the first woman to be elected to the British Parliament?

16 July 1945

In which country was the first atomic bomb detonated?

Birthdays	
16 July 1872	Roald Amundsen, Norwegian explorer
17 July 1899	James Cagney, American actor

17 July 1938

Douglas "Wrong-Way" Corrigan told the American authorities he wanted to fly to California, but where did he fly to instead?

17 July 1951

Which Dublin theatre burned down on this date?

18 July 1877
Who invented the phonograph or record-player?

18 July 1955
Which famous fun park opened at Anaheim, Los Angeles, on this date?

Birthdays	
18 July 1921	John Glenn, American astronaut and senator
18 July 1950	Richard Branson, British businessman and adventurer

19 July 1814
Name the American who invented the pistol with the revolving chamber.

Birthdays	
20 July 1919	Edmund Hillary, New Zealand mountain climber
20 July 1939	Diana Rigg, British actress

20 July 1944
Who narrowly escaped death during an explosion at his bunker in eastern Germany?

20 July 1982
Which terrorist group was responsible for the London explosions that killed eleven people and seven horses?

21 July 1796
At what early age did Scottish poet Robert Burns die: 29, 34, or 37?

21 July 1899

What was the subject matter of Ernest Hemingway's Spanish-based novel *Death in the Afternoon*?

21 July 1928

Which of John B. Keane's plays was made into a film with Richard Harris as the principal actor?

21 July 1969

Why did so many people watch Neil Armstrong taking a stroll along the Sea of Tranquillity?

21 July 1976

What position did British diplomat Christopher Ewart-Biggs hold at the time of his assassination?

23 July 1693

Which famous Irishman who defended Limerick in 1690 and 1691 is supposed to have said, "Oh, that this were for Ireland!" as he lay dying on a French battlefield?

23 July 1803

Who organised an abortive rising five years after 1798?

23 July 1980

Which actor will be forever associated with the role of Insp. Clouseau in the "Pink Panther" films?

23 July 1986

Which English royal wedding took place on this date but ended in failure six years later?

24 July 1802

Who wrote *The Three Musketeers* and *The Count of Monte Cristo*?

25 July 1554
Queen Mary of England married King Felipe (Philip) of Spain. Was this couple Protestant or Catholic?

25 July 1909
Who was the first person to fly the English Channel?

26 July 1856
Did George Bernard Shaw prefer to be called George or Bernard?

27 July 1980
The deposed Shah of Iran died in which north African country?

28 July 1586
Who introduced the potato to Ireland?

Birthdays	
28 July 1866	Beatrix Potter, British children's writer
28 July 1895	John Charles McQuaid, Archbishop of Dublin
29 July 1883	Benito Mussolini, dictator of Italy

29 July 1890
Which impoverished Dutch artist took his own life on this date?

29 July 1948
Where were the first Olympic Games held after the Second World War?

29 July 1955
Which show, presented by Éamonn Andrews, first appeared on British television on this date?

29 July 1981

In which London church did Prince Charles and Lady Diana Spencer marry?

30 July 1863

Which car manufacturer, born on this date, had a son named Edsel who died before him?

30 July 1930

Uruguay 4, Argentina 2. Where was the first World Cup final held?

30 July 1958

Which soft drinks company used Daley Thompson in their advertisements?

30 July 1966 (a)

England 4, Germany 2. Where did England achieve its only World Cup victory?

30 July 1966 (b)

What was Geoff Hurst's unique accomplishment during that World Cup final?

31 July 1556

Which religious order was founded by Iñigo de Oñez y Loyola (Ignatius of Loyola)?

31 July 1917

Which poet from Slane, Co. Meath, was killed in action during the First World War?

31 July 1975

The members of which famous showband were murdered near Newry, Co. Down?

August

1 August 1779
What is the name of the American national anthem?

1 August 1914
In the sequence of events leading up to the First World War, which country declared war on Russia?

2 August 1876
Which card player was shot in the back by Jack McCall in Deadwood, South Dakota?

2 August 1990
Which dictator ordered his troops to invade Kuwait?

3 August 1492
Who set sail for India but never got there?

3 August 1916
Which 1916 hero was executed about three months after the other leaders?

4 August 1900

Elizabeth Bowes-Lyon is the mother of which prominent member of the British royal family?

4 August 1914

At the beginning of the First World War, did Britain declare war on Germany or did Germany declare war on Britain?

Birthdays	
4 August 1792	Percy Bysshe Shelley, English poet
5 August 1906	John Huston, American film director
5 August 1930	Neil Armstrong, first person on the Moon

5 August 1958

Which American submarine was the first to pass under the North Pole?

5 August 1962

"Goodbye, Norma Jean" is Elton John's tribute to which American actress?

5 August 1984

Richard Jenkins, a Welsh actor and former husband of Elizabeth Taylor, was better known by what name?

6 August 1775

Which Irish statesman was known as the Liberator?

6 August 1945

What kind of object was dropped on Japan from an American plane named *Enola Gay*?

6 August 1978

The family name of the Pope who died on this date was Montini. Who was he?

7 August 1903

On which continent did Louis and Mary Leakey discover evidence of the earliest humans, including a 1,750,000-year-old skull?

8 August 1961

Dave Evans is a member of which rock band?

8 August 1963

Crime paid for Ronald Biggs. What did he rob?

8 August 1974

Which President of the United States was forced to resign over the Watergate scandal?

8 August 1991

What is the profession of John McCarthy, one of the Beirut hostages who was released on this date?

8 August 1992

Who was the first Irish person to win an Olympic gold medal since Ronnie Delaney's success in 1956?

9 August 1945

Because of bad weather, an atomic bomb could not be dropped on the Japanese city of Kokura. Which city was second choice for the bombers?

9 August 1974

Name the only President of the United States never elected to office.

10 August 1984

Where did American athlete Mary Decker trip on the heels of South African Zola Budd?

Birthdays	
11 August 1897	Enid Blyton, British children's writer
11 August 1921	Alex Haley, Black American writer

12 August 1908

What was the name of the Ford car that first rolled off an assembly line on this date?

13 August 1860

Which woman sharpshooter toured with Buffalo Bill's Wild West Show?

13 August 1899

In which country was film director Alfred Hitchcock born?

13 August 1961

What did the Soviet Union do in Berlin on Fidel Castro's 34th birthday?

14 August 1961

Singer Sarah Brightman was once married to which composer?

14 August 1969
On this date, where were British troops deployed for the first time?

15 August 1769
The Duke of Wellington and Napoleon were both born in 1769. Which of them was the older?

15 August 1771
Who wrote the novel *Ivanhoe*?

15 August 1914
Which President of the United States opened the Panama Canal?

Birthdays	
15 August 1888	T. E. Lawrence (Lawrence of Arabia), British soldier
15 August 1917	Jack Lynch, former Taoiseach
15 August 1919	Benedict Kiely, Irish writer
15 August 1950	Princess Anne, only daughter of Queen Elizabeth II

16 August 1896
The Klondike Gold Rush happened in which country?

16 August 1958
Which singer appeared in *Shanghai Surprise, Desperately Seeking Susan,* and *Dick Tracy*?

16 August 1977
Although several people claim to have seen him recently, which performer died in August 1977?

17 August 1920

Which red-haired film star played opposite John Wayne in
The Quiet Man?

17 August 1987

Rudolf Hess died in Spandau prison. In which city is this
prison?

19 August 1871

Which bicycle salesmen abandoned their business to
concentrate on making aeroplanes?

19 August 1887
Name the Irish poet who earned his living as a farm labourer and who was killed in Belgium during the First World War.

19 August 1977
What was the profession of Julius Marx?

19 August 1987
What did Michael Ryan do in the English town of Hungerford on this date?

19 August 1991
The American CNN television station beamed pictures of the abortive Soviet coup into homes throughout the world. What does CNN stand for?

20 August 1940
Josef Stalin ordered the murder of his old rival Leon Trotsky. In which American country did the assassination take place?

21 August 1930
Is Princess Margaret older or younger than her sister, Elizabeth?

21 August 1959
Jack Lord starred in the television series "Hawaii Five-O". What was the significance of the "five-o"?

22 August 1911
The Louvre museum in Paris was embarrassed by the theft of which famous painting on this date?

22 August 1922
Where in Co. Cork was Michael Collins killed?

22 August 1957
Who was the first professional snooker player to have a maximum break of 147 recorded on film?

23 August 1926

Which silent screen lover died on this date?

24 August 79

Volcanic ash from the eruption of which volcano buried the Roman towns of Pompeii and Herculaneum?

24 August 1990

Which Irishman set out for home from Beirut on this date?

25 August 1875

Matthew Webb was the first person to swim which large body of water?

25 August 1882

Which future President of Ireland was with Patrick Pearse in the GPO during the 1916 Rising?

25 August 1930

Seán Connery, the original James Bond, starred in which of the "Indiana Jones" films?

25 August 1944

Which capital city was liberated peacefully by the Allies in August 1944?

25 August 1954

English singer Declan McManus is better known by what name?

26 August 1819 (a)

Which of Prince Albert's children became King of England?

26 August 1819 (b)

Who was Prince Albert's wife?

26 August 1959
Sir Alec Issigonis designed which classic car for the British Motor Corporation?

26 August 1978
What job did Albino Luciani of Venice hold for thirty-three days?

27 August 1882 (a)
Sam Goldwyn said, "In two words: im possible" and "You can include me out." In which industry did this wit work?

27 August 1882 (b)
In the film world, what does MGM stand for?

27 August 1883
The eruption of which volcano between Java and Sumatra was heard 2,000 kilometres (3,000 miles) away?

27 August 1908
Which Texas-born politician made it to the White House in 1963?

27 August 1910
Which nun, born of Albanian parents, received part of her education in Ireland before undertaking work in India?

27 August 1957
Golfer Bernhard Langer is a native of which country?

27 August 1979
Which British elder statesman was murdered by the IRA in Co. Sligo?

28 August 1828
Which war did Leo Tolstoy write about in *War and Peace*?

28 August 1988
John Huston's last film, *The Dead*, was based on a short story by which Irish writer?

29 August 1871
Was artist Jack B. Yeats older or younger than his brother William?

29 August 1877
Brigham Young was the leader of which religious group based in Salt Lake City, Utah?

29 August 1949
In which film, set in America after the Civil War, did Richard Gere star with Jodie Foster?

29 August 1958
Two famous black men were born on 29 August 1958, one British and one American. Name either.

29 August 1975
What age was Éamon de Valera when he died: 90, 92, or 95?

30 August 1870
The first Montessori school was opened in which country in 1907?

31 August 1945
Van Morrison was born in which Irish city?

31 August 1986
The English sculptor Henry Moore has a piece commemorating William Butler Yeats in which Dublin city park?

SEPTEMBER

1 September 1715
Which King Louis of France was known as "the Sun King"?

Birthdays
1 September 1864   Roger Casement, Irish patriot
1 September 1875   Edgar Rice Burroughs,
                                 American author (*Tarzan*)

---

1 September 1939
Germany's invasion of which country finally sparked off the Second World War?

1 September 1985
Scientist Robert Ballard found the wreck of which famous ship off the coast of Newfoundland?

2 September 1666
Which capital city was devastated by a fire that started in Pudding Lane?

2 September 1937
Which sporting movement was founded by Frenchman Baron Pierre de Coubertin?

2 September 1945
Who formally surrendered to Gen. Douglas MacArthur on board the American warship *Missouri*?

2 September 1952
How many times did Jimmy Connors win the men's singles tennis championship at Wimbledon?

2 September 1973
Who wrote *The Lord of the Rings* and *The Hobbit*?

2 September 1980
Cancer victim Terry Fox attempted to run across North America to raise money for research, but his illness forced him to abandon the attempt shortly after the half-way mark. Was Terry Fox from Canada or the United States?

3 September 1658
Which Lord Protector of Britain and slaughterer of Irish people died on this date?

3 September 1783
Which war of independence was officially concluded with the Treaty of Paris?

3 September 1939
Name any one of the four countries that declared war on Germany on 3 September 1939.

3 September 1967
On which side of the road do people drive in Sweden?

4 September 1886
Which Apache warrior surrendered in Arizona and died peacefully in Oklahoma twenty-three years later?

4 September 1989
The French novelist Georges Simenon created which detective character?

5 September 1820
Which Irish educational order received Papal recognition on this date?

5 September 1847

Jesse James once delivered mail for which American enterprise?

5 September 1972

At which Olympic Games did terrorists take Israeli athletes hostage?

5 September 1982

What handicap had British Second World War pilot Douglas Bader?

Birthdays	
6 September 1888	Joe Kennedy, Boston financier and father of President John F. Kennedy
6 September 1942	Britt Ekland, Swedish actress
7 September 1533	Queen Elizabeth I, daughter of King Henry VIII and Anne Boleyn
7 September 1936	Buddy Holly, American singer

7 September 1981

Which Irish disabled writer died on this date?

8 September 1504

The famous Renaissance statue of David was carved by which artist?

8 September 1925

Which actor, normally associated with "Pink Panther" films, played several roles in *Dr Strangelove*?

9 September 1976

Which revolutionary leader founded Communist China?

9 September 1978

Martina Navratilova, who defected to the United States, is a native of which country?

10 September 1898

Name the husband-and-wife scientist team who discovered radium.

11 September 1649

The inhabitants of which Irish town were butchered by Oliver Cromwell on this date?

11 September 1917

Which woman, famous for having thousands of shoes, is the widow of Ferdinand Marcos?

11 September 1971

Nikita Khrushchev was Soviet leader from 1953 to 1964. Name either the leader before Khrushchev or the one immediately after him.

Birthdays
11 September 1885   D. H. Lawrence, British writer
11 September 1917   Ferdinand Marcos,
                            Philippine dictator

---

12 September 1953

Which American politician did Jacqueline Lee-Bouvier marry?

12 September 1977

Richard Attenborough's film *Cry Freedom* was based on the life and death of Steve Biko, who died in police custody. In what country did these events take place?

13 September 1793
James Hoban, who designed Washington's White House, was a native of which Irish county?

14 September 1916
During which drawn-out battle of the First World War were tanks first used?

14 September 1982
Which American-born European princess died after a car crash?

15 September 1789
Which novel by James Fenimore Cooper was made into a film starring Daniel Day-Lewis?

15 September 1890
Which writer created Miss Marple and Hercule Poirot?

16 September 1620
Name the ship that carried the Pilgrim Fathers to America.

16 September 1945
What title was bestowed on John McCormack by Pope Pius XI in 1928?

17 September 1977
Maria Callas was famous in which branch of the arts?

18 September 1709

Samuel Johnson, the English writer, was also a lexicographer. What is a lexicographer? (If you don't know, look up your dictionary.)

20 September 1519

Who captained the first ship to circumnavigate the world?

20 September 1580

Who captained the first English ship to circumnavigate the world?

20 September 1803

Which Irish revolutionary is more famous for his speech from the dock than for his rebellion?

20 September 1934
Sophia Loren was born in which Italian city?

20 September 1957
What nationality was the composer Jean Sibelius?

20 September 1967
Which luxury liner was launched at Clydebank, Scotland, on this date?

21 September 1866
Which H. G. Wells story was very effectively adapted for radio by Orson Welles?

21 September 1931 (a)
Who played the role of J. R. Ewing in the television series "Dallas"?

21 September 1931 (b)
What did the J. R. of J. R. Ewing stand for?

Birthdays	
21 September 1881	Éamonn Ceannt, 1916 Rising leader
21 September 1931	Larry Hagman, American actor
21 September 1934	Leonard Cohen, Canadian singer

22 September 1980
Which long-running war broke out in the Middle East on this date?

23 September 1949
Which American singer had a hit with "Born in the USA"?

24 September 1786

Which Italian-Irish businessman established a successful carriage transport business in the last century?

24 September 1942

In which country was Linda McCartney born?

25 September 1944

The father has been a Roman slave, a Dutch painter, and a cowboy; the son has been a policeman, a policeman, and a corrupt businessman. What is the family name of these American actors?

25 September 1952

What film role will Christopher Reeve always be associated with?

26 September 1888

Which Andrew Lloyd Weber musical is based on some of the poetry of T. S. Eliot?

26 September 1948

Which Australian singer represented Britain in the Eurovision Song Contest and played opposite John Travolta in the film *Grease*?

28 September 1891
Who wrote *Moby Dick*?

28 September 1895

Which French scientist is remembered for his work with bacteria and has a milk preservation technique named after him?

28 September 1978

After being elected Pope, what name did Albino Luciani take for himself?

29 September 1547

Which character, created by Miguel de Cervantes, fought windmills?

29 September 1758

Which English naval hero suffered from seasickness all his life?

29 September 1900

Who did Irishwoman Constance Gore-Booth marry on this date?

29 September 1935

Which loud American country-and-western singer sings "Goodness, gracious, great balls of fire"?

29 September 1979

Which head of state was greeted by millions of people when he stopped in Ireland for a couple of days on his way to America?

30 September 1900

Which Irish wit, on his death-bed in Paris, is reputed to have looked at the shabby wallpaper and said, "One of us has got to go"?

30 September 1938

After speaking to Hitler in Munich in 1938, what did British Prime Minister Neville Chamberlain promise his fellow-citizens?

30 September 1955

Which cult film star, who appeared in only three films, was killed while driving his sports car?

OCTOBER

1 October 1917

Who succeeded Cardinal Ó Fiaich as Archbishop of Armagh?

1 October 1969

Did the Concorde break the sound barrier for the first time over Britain or over France?

Birthdays	
1 October 1920	Walter Matthau, American actor
1 October 1924	Jimmy Carter, President of the United States
2 October 1869	Mohandas Gandhi, Indian statesman
2 October 1904	Graham Greene, British writer

2 October 1909

Where on the outskirts of London was the first Rugby Union football match played?

2 October 1985

What illness killed American film star Rock Hudson?

3 October 1226

Which religious order was founded by Giovanni Francesco Bernardone, the son of a wealthy merchant from Assisi?

3 October 1975 (a)

Dr Tiede Herrema, who was kidnapped near Limerick on this date, is a native of which European country?

3 October 1975 (b)

Where was Dr Herrema found and finally released after a long siege?

3 October 1990

Who was Chancellor (Prime Minister) of Germany when the country was reunified on this date?

4 October 1895

Which silent film star had a hit with *The General*?

4 October 1957 (a)

What was the name of the first artificial satellite launched into space?

4 October 1957 (b)

Which country launched the first artificial earth satellite?

5 October 1954

Which Irish-born singer was nominated for the Nobel Peace Prize for his work in bringing aid to Africa?

5 October 1968

A civil rights clash marked the beginning of the current Northern Ireland troubles. In which city did this initial clash take place?

6 October 1891

Which great Irish politician died in Brighton on this date?

6 October 1914

What nationality is explorer Thor Heyerdahl?

6 October 1981

Irish politician James Tully witnessed the assassination of which Egyptian leader?

7 October 1919

The world's first airline was launched in the Netherlands. What is the name of this airline, which is still in business?

7 October 1985

The cruise ship *Achille Lauro*, which was hijacked by Palestinian terrorists, belonged to which Mediterranean country?

Birthdays

7 October 1900	Heinrich Himmler, head of the Gestapo
7 October 1931	Desmond Tutu, South African bishop
8 October 1941	Rev. Jesse Jackson, American politician

---

8 October 1871

When Mrs O'Leary's cow knocked over an oil lamp, which American city was burned down?

9 October 1776

Which Californian city was founded on this date by Spanish missionaries?

9 October 1940

Which of the Beatles decided it was all right to wear his glasses on stage because Buddy Holly in America was wearing his?

11 October 1809

Which continent was explored by Lewis and Clark?

12 October 1492

Which group of islands did Christopher Columbus first encounter in the New World?

12 October 1975

Which pope canonised Oliver Plunkett on this date?

12 October 1984 (a)

In which English resort town did an IRA bomb nearly kill the entire British cabinet?

12 October 1984 (b)

Who was the Prime Minister of Britain at the time of that IRA bombing?

Birthdays
12 October 1935	Luciano Pavarotti,	Italian tenor
13 October 1925	Margaret Thatcher,	British politician
13 October 1941	Paul Simon,	American songwriter

---

13 October 1941

Paul Simon's early career was in partnership with which American singer?

14 October 1066

Which Norman leader defeated the Saxons at the Battle of Hastings?

14 October 1882

Which Irish politician with a Spanish father was born in New York?

14 October 1890

During the 1950s, Richard Nixon was Vice-President to which former war hero?

14 October 1940

Which enduring British singer has remained popular since first reaching stardom in the late 1950s?

14 October 1944

Who killed Nazi general Erwin Rommel?

14 October 1947

Which technological barrier was first broken by Chuck Yeager on this date?

14 October 1977

What sporting activity was Bing Crosby involved in when he died suddenly?

15 October 1881

Name the comical butler created by author P. G. Wodehouse.

16 October 1793

Which Austrian-born Queen of France was guillotined during the French Revolution?

16 October 1815

To where was Napoleon finally sent in exile?

16 October 1854

Was Oscar Wilde born in Westland Row, Malahide, or London?

16 October 1886

David Ben-Gurion was the first Prime Minister of which modern state?

16 October 1890

To which document was Michael Collins referring when he said that he had signed his death warrant?

16 October 1925 (a)

Who is the star of the television series "Murder She Wrote"?

16 October 1925 (b)

What is the name of the character played by the star of "Murder She Wrote"?

16 October 1978

Where in the Vatican do the cardinals meet to elect a new pope?

Birthdays	
16 October 1888	Eugene O'Neill, American dramatist
16 October 1890	Michael Collins, Irish soldier and statesman

17 October 1849

With what musical instrument will Chopin always be associated?

17 October 1931

What charge finally landed Al Capone in jail?

17 October 1973

What weapon was used by Arab states against the western world in 1973?

17 October 1979

In which Indian city has Mother Teresa her headquarters?

18 October 1931

What kind of sensory handicap did inventor Thomas Edison have to tolerate for most of his life?

18 October 1956

How many times has Martina Navratilova won the Wimbledon women's singles tennis title?

18 October 1989

Which city endured a major earthquake in 1906 and another serious one on this date?

19 October 1745

Which clergyman used to appear on one of Ireland's banknotes?

19 October 1781

During the American War of Independence, Gen. Cornwallis surrendered at Yorktown to which famous American leader?

19 October 1931

David Cornwell, who wrote *The Spy Who Came In from the Cold* and *Smiley's People*, is better known by what pen name?

Birthdays

20 October 1632	Sir Christopher Wren, British architect
20 October 1822	Thomas Hughes, British writer (*Tom Brown's Schooldays*)

---

21 October 1805

Who won the Battle of Trafalgar, although he died in action?

21 October 1833

What product made Alfred Nobel's fortune for him?

21 October 1904
Which Monaghan-born poet has a bench in his memory on the bank of the Grand Canal in Dublin?

21 October 1917
Jazz musician Dizzie Gillespie was associated with which musical instrument?

21 October 1956
Carrie Fisher played the role of Princess Leia in which hugely successful film?

21 October 1966
When a coal slag-heap engulfed the village school in Aberfan, 144 people, including 116 children, perished. Is Aberfan in England, Scotland, or Wales?

21 October 1973
Which opera house in the Southern Hemisphere was officially opened by Queen Elizabeth II?

Birthdays
21 October 1772   Samuel Taylor Coleridge, British poet

---

22 October 1811
Franz Liszt was a native of which European country?

23 October 1921
Although many people think he invented it, what product was not first invented by John Boyd Dunlop?

23 October 1940
Which Brazilian soccer star scored over a thousand goals during his professional career?

23 October 1987
Which famous jockey ended up in jail for tax evasion?

24 October 1929
Which famous financial collapse began on this date?

24 October 1936
Bill Wyman is a member of which long-running British rock group?

25 October 1825
Which composer, better known for his waltzes, wrote the opera *Die Fledermaus*?

25 October 1854
What historic incident happened at Balaklava during the Crimean War?

25 October 1960
Sir Harry Ferguson teamed up with Henry Ford to build what kind of machine?

Birthdays
25 October 1881   Pablo Picasso, Spanish artist

---

26 October 1881 (a)
Billy Claibourne, the Clanton brothers and the McLowery brothers were the bad guys at this gunfight; the Earp brothers and Doc Holliday were the good guys. Where did this memorable shoot-out take place?

26 October 1881 (b)
What kind of doctor was gunfighter Doc Holliday?

27 October 1939
Which lanky British comedian is noted for his silly walks and his appearance in the film *A Fish Called Wanda*?

27 October 1971
What was the African country Zaïre called at one time?

27 October 1978
The head of which state shared the 1978 Nobel Peace Prize with Egypt's Anwar al-Sadat?

28 October 1886
Which gift from France to the United States was inaugurated in New York Harbour?

28 October 1958
How many Pope Johns were there before the elderly Cardinal Angelo Roncalli was made pope on this date?

29 October 1618

Which potato-eating, cigar-smoking coffee-drinker was a popular member of the court of Queen Elizabeth I of England but was beheaded fifteen years after her death?

29 October 1897

Who was Hitler's Minister for Propaganda: Goebbels, Göring, or Himmler?

29 October 1929

Which financial market finally collapsed on Black Tuesday in October 1929?

29 October 1949

Which Steven Spielberg film featured Richard Dreyfuss as a wealthy oceanographer?

30 October 1926

Which escape artist and magician could take a heavy blow to the stomach but died after somebody hit him when he wasn't ready?

30 October 1932

French film director Louis Malle is married to the main character of the American television series "Murphy Brown". Who is she?

30 October 1938

People tuning their radios to Orson Welles's "Invasion from Mars" were convinced they were being invaded and fled their homes. In which country did these events happen?

30 October 1979

What device did Sir Barnes Wallis develop to assist the British Air Force in destroying dams in Germany?

30 October 1984
Which Prime Minister of India was assassinated by her own trusted Sikh bodyguards?

31 October 1517
Who started the Reformation by nailing ninety-five theses (arguments) on a church door at Wittenberg?

31 October 1795
Which romantic poet wrote *Ode to a Nightingale* and *Ode on a Grecian Urn*?

31 October 1961
Which member of U2 was the one who originally advertised on his school notice-board for like-minded musicians?

31 October 1971
An IRA bomb badly damaged the post office tower in which British city?

November

1 November 1625
St Oliver Plunkett was archbishop of which diocese?

1 November 1884
Name the hotel in Thurles where the GAA was founded.

1 November 1920
Which 18-year-old medical student was hanged for his part in an ambush on a British military lorry?

1 November 1976
Peanut farmer Jimmy Carter was elected President of the United States on this date. Was he a Republican or Democrat?

1 November 1988

Following market research among its readers, DC Comics arranged the killing off by the Joker of which character?

2 November 1734

Which frontiersman founded a settlement now known as Boonesboro?

2 November 1913

Which American actor was an oil baron in the film *Local Hero* and a convicted murderer in *The Birdman of Alcatraz*?

2 November 1950

Major Barbara and *Pygmalion* were written by which Irish Nobel Prize winner?

3 November 1871

Name the two nineteenth-century Europeans who met for the first time in the wilderness of Africa.

3 November 1921

Which tough-guy actor played the leading role in the "Death Wish" films?

3 November 1923

Cardinal Tomás Ó Fiaich came from which Co. Armagh village?

3 November 1957

What claim to fame had Soviet dog Laika?

4 November 1884

Which tractor manufacturer was the first person to fly a plane in Ireland?

4 November 1979

The staff of which embassy were taken hostages by Iranian students?

4 November 1980
Who was the oldest President of the United States?

4 November 1985
The first Director-General of RTE achieved fame while working for British television. Who was he?

5 November 1605
Guy Fawkes's gunpowder plot failed, but which English institution was he trying to blow up?

5 November 1991
Which newspaper proprietor died when he fell overboard from his private yacht close to the Canary Islands?

5 November 1913
What was Vivien Leigh's most memorable film role?

Birthdays
6 November 1892   Sir John Alcock, British aviator
7 November 1867   Marie Curie, Polish-French scientist
7 November 1913   Albert Camus, French writer

---

7 November 1975
Which Dutch businessman was kidnapped in Limerick and released after a siege in Monasterevin?

8 November 1656
Which celestial body, named after Edmund Halley, is featured on the Bayeux Tapestry?

8 November 1900
In which city did *Gone with the Wind* writer Margaret Mitchell live?

8 November 1922

In which country did Dr Christiaan Barnard perform the first human heart transplant?

8 November 1987

Where did the IRA plant a bomb, killing civilians who were attending a memorial service for the dead of the First World War?

9 November 1875

Which Irish art collector changed his mind about leaving his paintings to Britain, but died before he was able to make his change of heart legal?

9 November 1922

By what initials was Germany's Schutzstaffel (Protective Squadron) better known?

9 November 1926

Jack Keyes-Byrne is the real name of which Irish dramatist?

9 November 1938

Who were the victims of Kristallnacht (Glass Night), when German citizens went on the rampage, smashing windows and killing people?

9 November 1970

Which former President of France died exactly ten years after John F. Kennedy was elected President of the United States?

10 November 1879

The portrait of which 1916 leader is usually a side view or profile?

10 November 1925

In what country was coalminer's son Richard Burton born?

10 November 1982

In the few years between Leonid Brezhnev's death and Gorbachev's leadership, how many leaders had the Soviet Union?

11 November 1918

Which war ended on the eleventh hour of the eleventh day of the eleventh month?

11 November 1940

What is the shortened name of the general-purpose vehicle issued to the US Army during the Second World War?

12 November 1961

Which Romanian gymnast achieved a perfect score and won three gold medals at the 1976 Olympic Games?

Birthdays

12 November 1840	Auguste Rodin, French sculptor
12 November 1929	Grace Kelly (Princess Grace of Monaco), American actress
12 November 1961	Nadia Comanech, Romanian gymnast
13 November 1850	Robert Louis Stevenson, Scottish writer

---

13 November 1985

In which country did Pope John Paul II pray at the base of the Nevado del Ruíz volcano which had erupted, killing and burying about 25,000 people?

13 November 1987

Dutch war criminal Pieter Menten had a home at Lemybrien in which Munster county?

117

14 November 1180

St Lorcán Ó Tuathail was bishop of which Irish city?

14 November 1948

On 14 November 1948, who became second in line for the British throne?

15 November 1864

Towards the end of the American Civil War, Gen. William Sherman destroyed which city in Georgia?

15 November 1891

Which German general, beaten by Montgomery in northern Africa, was involved in the plot to assassinate Hitler?

15 November 1956

Which famous American singer had his first film part in *Love Me Tender*?

15 November 1985

Margaret Thatcher signed the Anglo-Irish Agreement on behalf of the British Government. Which Taoiseach signed it on behalf of the Irish Government?

16 November 1960

Which actor played opposite Vivien Leigh in *Gone with the Wind* and opposite Marilyn Monroe in *The Misfits*?

16 November 1961

Name the soft-spoken British boxer who managed to win both the British and European heavyweight titles.

17 November 1869

Ferdinand de Lesseps, who built the Suez Canal, was a native of which European country?

17 November 1974

Who was the only President of Ireland to die in office?

Birthdays

Birthdays

17 November 1887	Field-Marshal Bernard Montgomery, British Second World War commander
17 November 1925	Rock Hudson, American actor
17 November 1930	Brian Lenihan, Irish politician
17 November 1942	Martin Scorsese, American film director

18 November 1626
Which big church in Rome was consecrated on this date?

18 November 1987
What kind of disaster happened at King's Cross underground railway station, London?

18 November 1991
Name the Archbishop of Canterbury's special envoy who was held hostage in Beirut.

Birthdays

| 18 November 1836 | Sir William Gilbert, British lyricist |
| 18 November 1907 | Sir Alec Issigonis, Turkish-British car designer |

19 November 1798
Which Irish patriot committed suicide in his cell rather than give the British the satisfaction of hanging him?

19 November 1863
"Four score and seven years ago" are the first words of which memorable speech by Abraham Lincoln?

19 November 1977

Name the first Arab head of state to visit Israel.

Birthdays	
19 November 1805	Ferdinand de Lesseps, French promoter of the Suez Canal
19 November 1917	Indira Gandhi, Prime Minister of India
19 November 1962	Jodie Foster, American actress
20 November 1925	Robert F. Kennedy, American senator

20 November 1947

Which British monarch was great-great-grandmother of both Queen Elizabeth II and her husband, Prince Philip?

20 November 1975

Juan Carlos became King of Spain after the death of which dictator?

21 November 1974

How many people were jailed for the two Birmingham pub bombings?

Birthdays	
21 November 1694	François-Marie Arouet (Voltaire), French philosopher
21 November 1888	Arthur "Harpo" Marx, American comedian
21 November 1945	Goldie Hawn, American actress
22 November 1808	Thomas Cook, British travel agent

22 November 1718

By what name was pirate Edward Teach better known?

22 November 1913
Benjamin Britten made a contribution to which branch of the arts?

22 November 1943
Billie Jean King was a champion at which sport?

22 November 1946
What kind of convenient writing instrument went on sale in Britain on this date?

22 November 1963
In which city was John F. Kennedy assassinated?

22 November 1967
Which German tennis star was born exactly four years after Kennedy was assassinated?

22 November 1991
Many people will remember 22 November as the date President John F. Kennedy was killed. Why will Margaret Thatcher remember it?

23 November 1852
Which new idea for posting letters was first tried by the British post office in the Channel Islands?

23 November 1859
William Bonney, born in New York, went west to become a notorious outlaw. By what name was he better known?

24 November 1859
Which nineteenth-century scientist wrote *The Origin of Species*?

24 November 1942
Which alcohol-free lager was advertised by Billy Connolly?

24 November 1963
Who did Jack Ruby shoot in Dallas?

24 November 1991
Freddie Mercury, who died of AIDS, was the lead singer with which group?

Birthdays	
24 November 1864	Henri de Toulouse-Lautrec, French artist
24 November 1868	Scott Joplin, American ragtime composer
24 November 1942	Billy Connolly, Scottish comedian

25 November 1835
Did Scottish-American millionaire Andrew Carnegie make most of his money in iron and steel, oil, or textiles?

25 November 1844
The name of which early motor car pioneer, born on this date, still appears on cars today?

25 November 1914
Which platinum-blonde actress married baseball star Joe Di Maggio?

25 November 1952
Which long-running play by Agatha Christie opened on this date?

25 November 1974
Burmese statesman U Thant was once the Secretary-General of which international organisation?

25 November 1984

What was the name of the original song recorded by Bob Geldof and several other stars to raise money for famine relief in Africa?

26 November 1910

Which actor played the role of Uncle Peter in the RTE series "Glenroe"?

26 November 1922 (a)

Which cartoon strip was created by Charles Schulz?

26 November 1922 (b)

Tutankhamun was not an important pharaoh, but why was the finding of his tomb significant?

26 November 1939

Which energetic Black American singer had a hit with "Private Dancer"?

27 November 1921

Alexander Dubcek tried to reform his country in the 1960s but the Soviet Union stopped him by invading the country in 1968. In which country was Dubcek prime minister?

Birthdays

27 November 1701	Anders Celsius, Swedish scientist who developed the Celsius (centigrade) temperature scale.
27 November 1942	Jimi Hendrix, American singer and guitarist
28 November 1757	William Blake, English illustrator and poet
29 November 1832	Louisa May Alcott, American children's writer (*Little Women*)

---

30 November 1667
On which banknote was there a portrait of Jonathan Swift?

30 November 1835
What pen name, derived from seamen's depth-sounding jargon on the Mississippi, did Samuel Langhorne Clemens use?

30 November 1874
Which Prime Minister of Britain won the Nobel Prize for Literature?

30 November 1967
Patrick Kavanagh, who died on this date, was a native of which county?

DECEMBER

1 December 1935
Which American comedian made the films *Bananas, Play It Again, Sam,* and *Annie Hall*?

1 December 1939
Lee Trevino, who survived being struck by lightning, was a champion at which sport?

1 December 1989
Name the Soviet leader who met Pope John Paul II in the Vatican.

1 December 1990
What was significant about a French worker shaking the hand of a British worker on this date?

2 December 1697

Which masterpiece by Sir Christopher Wren crowned London after reconstruction following the 1666 fire was completed?

2 December 1804

Who literally crowned himself Emperor of France?

2 December 1859

Was American activist John Brown pro-slavery or anti-slavery?

2 December 1982

What kind of artificial organ, powered by compressed air, worked inside Barney Clark for a few months?

3 December 1552

Which Japanese city, later to be an atomic bomb target, was home to a Christian mission founded by St Francisco Javier (Francis Xavier)?

3 December 1894

Which Scottish writer died on the South Pacific island of Samoa?

3 December 1967

Louis Washkanski was the first person to have a heart transplant. In which African country did he have the operation?

3 December 1984

A chemical leak from a Union Carbide factory in the city of Bhopal killed about three thousand people. In which country is Bhopal?

Birthdays	
3 December 1857	Joseph Conrad, Polish-English writer
3 December 1901	Walt Disney, American cartoon film producer
3 December 1930	Andy Williams, American singer
3 December 1930	Jean-Luc Godard, French film director

4 December 1154

What nationality was Nicholas Breakspear, who became Pope Adrian IV?

4 December 1872

What was the name of the ship that was found mysteriously abandoned but totally intact in the North Atlantic?

4 December 1937

Which comic, featuring Korky the Cat, was first published on this date?

Birthdays	
4 December 1892	Gen. Francisco Franco, Spanish dictator
4 December 1949	Jeff Bridges, American actor

5 December 1594

Mercator was a cartographer. What did he make?

5 December 1791

Which musical genius is buried in an unmarked grave in Vienna?

5 December 1839

Which American general was killed by Sioux warriors in June 1876?

5 December 1933

In the United States, what did Prohibition forbid people from doing?

5 December 1979

Who resigned as Taoiseach on this date?

6 December 1921

Was the partition treaty, setting up the Irish Free State, signed in Dublin or London?

6 December 1946

José Carreras bravely resumed his singing career after fighting which disease?

6 December 1988

Which 1950s and 1960s blind singer died while trying to make a come-back in the 1980s?

7 December 1817

Which harsh sea captain survived a mutiny on his ship in 1789 and died on this date?

7 December 1941

Which incident brought the United States into the Second World War?

7 December 1988

Which country suffered a severe earthquake, killing about 100,000 inhabitants?

7 December 1991

Which mediaeval Croatian city, considered a world heritage site, was bombed by Serbian forces?

8 December 1542

Who died first, Mary Queen of Scots or Queen Elizabeth I?

8 December 1980

Which singer was murdered by Mark David Chapman?

Birthdays	
8 December 1925	Sammy Davis Junior, American comedian
8 December 1943	Jim Morrison, American 1960s singer (the Doors)

9 December 1967

Which man ruled Romania from 1967 until his death in 1989?

9 December 1990

Which trade union leader was elected President of Poland?

Birthdays	
9 December 1608	John Milton, blind English poet
9 December 1886	Clarence Birdseye, American developer of frozen food
9 December 1918	Kirk Douglas, American actor

10 December 1830

What nationality was poet Emily Dickinson?

10 December 1896
Prizes in memory of which industrialist are awarded on the anniversary of his death each year?

11 December 1905
Which future President of Ireland was born in London on this date?

11 December 1918
What is author Aleksandr Solzhenitsyn's home country, from which he was expelled in 1974?

11 December 1936
Having announced his decision on 10 December 1936, what did King Edward VIII do on the following day?

11 December 1979
Who became Taoiseach after the resignation of Jack Lynch?

12 December 1913
Which stolen priceless painting was discovered under a bed in Firenze (Florence)?

12 December 1915
Which singer-actor who describes himself as a Yankee from New Jersey had a hit with the song "My Way"?

12 December 1946
At what sport has Emerson Fittipaldi been a world champion?

12 December 1955
What kind of transport was patented by Christopher Cockerell on this date?

13 December 1925
In which film did Dick van Dyke drive a car that was able to fly?

13 December 1929

In which film did Christopher Plummer play the role of Count von Trapp, who married an ex-nun played by Julie Andrews?

Birthdays	
13 December 1925	Dick van Dyke, American actor
13 December 1929	Christopher Plummer, English actor

14 December 1911

At the South Pole, who did Roald Amundsen leave a note for?

Birthdays	
14 December 1503	Michel de Notre Dame (Nostradamus), French astrologer
14 December 1895	King George VI of England
14 December 1935	Lee Remick, American actress

15 December 1832

Which man, best known for his metal tower in Paris, designed the steel framework inside the Statue of Liberty?

15 December 1840

Who died in exile in 1821 and was buried in Paris in 1840?

15 December 1890

Which famous Sioux warrior was killed in a skirmish with the US army on this date?

15 December 1892

Which commodity made John Paul Getty very rich?

16 December 1770

Ludwig is the first name of which famous German composer?

16 December 1773
In which city in the American colonies did people launch a protest by dumping tea in a harbour?

16 December 1944
Which famous bandleader went missing over the English Channel towards the end of the Second World War?

Birthdays
16 December 1775   Jane Austen, English novelist
16 December 1889   Noel Coward, English dramatist

---

17 December 1778
Who invented a safety lamp for miners?

17 December 1857
What does the Beaufort Scale measure?

17 December 1903
Who made aviation history at Kitty Hawk, North Carolina?

Birthdays
17 December 1778   Sir Humphry Davy, English scientist
17 December 1936   Tommy Steele,
English actor and singer

---

18 December 1737
Which master violin maker died in Cremona, Italy?

18 December 1779
Which British clown had the same surname as the royal family of Monaco?

18 December 1919
How did Sir John Alcock die?

18 December 1947

What is the name of the biggest meat-eating dinosaur in Steven Spielberg's film *Jurassic Park*?

Birthdays

18 December 1916	Betty Grable, American actress
18 December 1943	Keith Richard, English rock star (Rolling Stones)
18 December 1947	Steven Spielberg, American film director

---

19 December 1923

Which actor played the role of Hudson the butler in the television series "Upstairs, Downstairs"?

Birthdays

19 December 1906	Leonid Brezhnev, Soviet leader
19 December 1922	Éamonn Andrews, Irish entertainer
19 December 1923	Gordon Jackson, Scottish actor

---

20 December 1952

Which one of these films did Jenny Agutter not star in: *The Railway Children, Logan's Run, Cabaret*?

20 December 1968

Henry Fonda starred in *The Grapes of Wrath*. Who wrote the original book?

21 December 1620

In which American state is the landing place of the *Mayflower*, which carried the Pilgrim Fathers from England?

21 December 1935

Which film company produced *Snow White*?

21 December 1940
Who wrote *The Great Gatsby?*

21 December 1945
How was American war hero Gen. George Patton killed?

21 December 1968
Which happened first, a person flying around the far side of the Moon or a person walking on the Moon?

21 December 1991
Which actress married CNN owner Ted Turner on her birthday?

Birthdays

21 December 1917	Heinrich Böll, German writer
21 December 1937	Jane Fonda, American actress
21 December 1954	Chris Evert, American tennis champion
22 December 1949	Maurice and Robin Gibb, English-born singers (the Bee-Gees)

---

22 December 1988
Flight 103, the Jumbo jet that blew up over Lockerbie, Scotland, belonged to which American airline?

23 December 1888
Which artist, after an argument with Paul Gauguin, cut off his own earlobe?

23 December 1912
Does Yousuf Karsh of Ottawa use a pencil, a brush or a camera for his portraits of famous people?

24 December 1491

What nationality was Iñigo de Oñez y Loyola (Ignatius of Loyola), founder of the Jesuits?

24 December 1601

At what battle did Lord Mountjoy defeat Aodh Ó Néill?

24 December 1871

Which Italian wrote the opera *Aida*, which opened Cairo's new Opera House on this date?

Birthdays

24 December 1809 Christopher (Kit) Carson, American frontiersman

24 December 1922 Ava Gardner, American actress

---

25 December 4 BC

Which world leader was born in this year?

25 December 1889

The star of the film *Casablanca* had a Christmas Day birthday. Who was he?

25 December 1977

Which famous comedian's body was kidnapped in Switzerland?

25 December 1989

Which tyrant and his wife were shot by firing squad after the citizens staged a revolution on this date?

26 December 1831

During the voyage of the *Beagle*, which scientist worked on his theory of evolution?

26 December 1972

Vice-President Harry Truman of the United States took over after the death of which president?

26 December 1989

Irish playwright Samuel Beckett generally wrote in which language?

Birthdays	
26 December 1893	Mao Zedong, leader of the Chinese communist revolution
26 December 1914	Richard Widmark, American actor

27 December 1904

The double bill *On Baile's Strand* by W. B. Yeats and *Spreading the News* by Lady Gregory marked the opening of which famous theatre?

27 December 1983

Who paid a visit to Mehmet Ali Agca in jail just after Christmas, 1983?

Birthdays	
27 December 1571	Johannes Kepler, German astronomer
27 December 1822	Louis Pasteur, French scientist
27 December 1901	Marlene Dietrich, German-American actress

28 December 1732

Sir Walter Scott wrote the novel *Rob Roy*, but was Rob Roy a real or fictitious character?

28 December 1949

"The next world war will be fought with stones." Which German-American scientist made this comment?

29 December 1170 (a)

In which cathedral was St Thomas Becket murdered?

29 December 1170 (b)

Which American-British poet wrote the play *Murder in the Cathedral*?

29 December 1986

Was Prime Minister Harold Macmillan of Britain a Conservative or Labour politician?

Birthdays	
29 December 1937	Mary Tyler Moore, American actress and film producer
29 December 1938	Jon Voight, American actor

30 December 1916

Which churchman, known as "the Mad Monk", had a strong influence over the Russian royal family, particularly the Tsarina Aleksandra?

30 December 1979

Which of the Rogers and Hammerstein team wrote the music and which wrote the lyrics?

Birthdays	
30 December 1865	Rudyard Kipling, English writer (born in India)
30 December 1959	Tracey Ullman, British comedian

31 December 1943

British actor Ben Kingsley won an Oscar for his role as which Indian political leader?

Birthdays

31 December 1869 Henri Matisse, French painter

31 December 1937 Anthony Hopkins, British actor

ANSWERS

1 January 1804
France.

1 January 1958
The European Economic Community (EEC).

1 January 1959
Fidel Castro.

1 January 1973
Ireland and Britain.

2 January 1492
Queen Isabella.

3 January 1924
Tutankhamun's tomb, discovered on this date.

3 January 1959
Alaska.

4 January 1986
Thin Lizzy.

5 January 1922
Sir Ernest Shackleton, who died on this date.

5 January 1981
Peter Sutcliffe, who was charged with the first of the murders on this date.

6 January 1412
Jeanne d'Arc (Joan of Arc).

6 January 1919
Theodore Roosevelt died on this date. Franklin Roosevelt did not die until 1945.

7 January 1844
St Bernadette.

7 January 1965
Jimmy O'Dea, who died on this date.

7 January 1975
Éamon de Valera's wife, Sinéad, died on this date.

8 January 1935
He was born in Mississippi, on this date.

8 January 1947
David Bowie, who was born on this date.

9 January 1913
Richard Nixon was born in California, on this date.

11 January 1928
Thomas Hardy, who died on this date.

12 January 1893
The Luftwaffe. The date is Göring's birthday.

12 January 1976
Agatha Christie.

13 January 1941
In Zürich, on this date.

14 January 1742
Halley's Comet.

14 January 1938
Snow White. The film went on general release on this date.

15 January 1929
Martin Luther King, who was born on this date.

16 January 1991
The Gulf War against Iraq began on this date.

17 January 1706
Benjamin Franklin, who was born on this date.

17 January 1860
Douglas Hyde, who was born on this date.

17 January 1874
They were Siamese twins. Joined together all their life, they died within three hours of each other. Chang meant "left" and Eng meant "right".

18 January 1892
Oliver Hardy.

18 January 1912
Robert Falcon Scott. They reached the South Pole on this date, only to find a note from Amundsen indicating that he made it before them.

19 January 1807
Gen. Robert E. Lee, who was born on this date.

19 January 1988
Christopher Nolan. He won the award on this date at the age of 22.

20 January 1936
King George V, who died on this date.

20 January 1961
John F. Kennedy, who was sworn in on this date.

20 January 1968
Sir Alfred Chester Beatty.

20 January 1981
Ronald Reagan, who was inaugurated on this date.

21 January 1793
King Louis XVI.

21 January 1876
Jim Larkin, who was born on this date.

21 January 1919
The Mansion House, where Dáil Éireann first met on this date.

21 January 1924
V. I. Lenin.

21 January 1925
Kojak, played by Telly Savalas, who was born on this date.

21 January 1976
Concorde. Flights by British Airways and Air France took off simultaneously.

22 January 1901
Queen Victoria, who died on this date.

22 January 1940
John Hurt, who was born on this date.

23 January 1989
Dali was a native of Spain. He died on this date.

24 January 1848
Marshall discovered gold on this date, leading to the 1849 Gold Rush to California.

24 January 1965
Sir Winston Churchill, who died on this date.

25 January 1759
Robert Burns, who was born on this date.

25 January 1874
William Somerset Maugham, who was born on this date.

25 January 1947
Al Capone, who died on this date.

26 January 1788
Australia celebrated its bicentennial on 26 January 1988, the 200th anniversary of the arrival of Capt. Arthur Phillip at Sydney.

26 January 1907
John Millington Synge. The date is that of the opening night of *The Playboy of the Western World*.

27 January 1756
Mozart was born in Salzburg on this date.

27 January 1832
Lewis Carroll, who was born on this date.

27 January 1868
"Dr Livingstone, I presume?" They met on this date.

27 January 1967 (a)
Sir Francis Chichester.

27 January 1967 (b)
Apollo 1. The oxygen-rich capsule went on fire on this date.

28 January 1841
Wales. Stanley (whose original name was John Rowlands) was born on this date.

28 January 1939
William Butler Yeats, who died on this date.

28 January 1986
She was killed in the space shuttle *Challenger* on this date, having been chosen to be the first ordinary American citizen in space.

29 January 1879
W. C. Fields (originally W. C. Dukinfield), who was born on this date.

30 January 1649
Oliver Cromwell. King Charles I was beheaded on this date.

30 January 1933
Adolf Hitler, who was appointed Chancellor on this date.

30 January 1948
Mohandas (Mahatma) Gandhi, who died on this date.

30 January 1972
Derry. The incident is now remembered as Bloody Sunday.

31 January 1943
Stalingrad. The Germans surrendered on this date after being worn down by the brave Russian fighters and the harsh Russian winter.

31 January 1951
Phil Collins, who was born on this date.

FEBRUARY

1 February
Bríd (Brigid).

1 February 1901
Clark Gable, who was born on this date.

1 February 1966
Buster Keaton, who died on this date.

1 February 1979
The Ayatollah Khomeini, who returned to Iran on this date.

2 February 1665
New York, which they captured on this date.

2 February 1709
Daniel Defoe's Robinson Crusoe.

2 February 1989
The Soviet Union.

3 February 1468
Johann Gutenberg, who died on this date.

3 February 1907
James Michener, who was born on this date.

4 February 1868
Gore-Booth. She was born on this date.

4 February 1902
Charles Lindbergh, who was born on this date.

4 February 1945
Josef Stalin. The Yalta Conference began on this date.

5 February 1945
Jamaica. Bob Marley was born on this date.

5 February 1989
Sky Television.

6 February 1952
Kenya. King George VI died on this date.

6 February 1958
Manchester United. The team had just qualified for the European Cup semi-finals following a match in Belgrade, and were flying home via Munich.

7 February 1867
Railways. He died on this date.

8 February 1587
Queen Elizabeth I. Mary Queen of Scots was beheaded on this date.

8 February 1931
James Dean, who was born on this date.

9 February 1923
Brendan Behan, who was born on this date.

9 February 1926
Garret FitzGerald, who was born on this date.

9 February 1969
The Boeing 747 or Jumbo Jet.

9 February 1983
Shergar, who was kidnapped on this date.

10 February 1837
Pushkin, who died on this date, was Russian.

10 February 1840
He married Queen Victoria of England, on this date.

10 February 1913
Capt. Robert Scott and his team. Their bodies were found on this date, only fifteen kilometres (ten miles) from their base and safety.

11 February 1847
Thomas Edison, who was born on this date, recorded "Mary Had a Little Lamb" when he was trying out his new invention, the phonograph.

11 February 1990
Nelson Mandela, who was released on this date.

12 February 1809 (a)
Abraham Lincoln, who was born on this date.

12 February 1809 (b)
Charles Darwin, who was born on this date.

13 February 1542
Catherine Howard, who died on this date, was the fifth wife of King Henry VIII.

14 February 1779
Capt. James Cook. He was killed by natives on Hawaii on this date.

14 February 1929
Al Capone. Seven gang members of Capone's rival Bugsy Moran were gunned down on this date.

14 February 1944
Alan Parker, who was born on this date.

14 February 1945
Dresden, heavily bombed on the night of 14/15 February.

14 February 1981
Artane.

15 February 1564
Galileo Galilei, who was born on this date.

15 February 1942
Singapore. The city was heavily defended against a sea attack but had weak northern defences, which the Japanese approached over land.

16 February 1959
John McEnroe, who was born on this date.

17 February 1909
Geronimo, who died on this date, was a member of the Apache tribe.

17 February 1922
It was the first stamp issued by the Irish Free State.

18 February 1517
Port Laoise, named Maryborough after Queen Mary Tudor, who was born on this date.

18 February 1546
Martin Luther, who died on this date.

18 February 1564
Michelangelo Buonarotti, who died on this date.

18 February 1930
Pluto was discovered on this date by Clyde Tombaugh (who knew where in the sky to look thanks to earlier calculations made by Percival Lowell, who died in 1916).

18 February 1932
Mozart. The director Milos Forman was born on this date.

18 February 1933
Seán. Yoko Ono was born in Tokyo on this date.

18 February 1954
The Bee-Gees. John Travolta was born on this date.

19 February 1473
Polish. He was born on this date.

19 February 1906
W. K. Kellogg, who founded his company on this date.

19 February 1924
The Terminator. Lee Marvin was born on this date.

19 February 1960
Charles and Anne. Prince Andrew was born on this date.

19 February 1982
The De Lorean Motor Company in Belfast.

20 February 1694
Voltaire (pen name of François-Marie Arouet), who was born on this date.

20 February 1927
Sidney Poitier, who was born on this date, was the first Black American to win the Best Actor award.

20 February 1962
John Glenn. He did so on this date.

21 February 1794
Antonio López de Santa Anna, who was born on this date.

21 February 1801
Cardinal John Henry Newman, who was born on this date.

21 February 1965
Malcolm X (original name Malcolm Little), who died on this date, was a Muslim.

21 February 1986
Izumi was 120, the world's oldest person. His age can be authenticated by Japan's first census of 1871, where he was recorded as a six-year-old.

22 February 1512
Amerigo Vespucci, who died on this date.

22 February 1732
George Washington, who was born on this date.

22 February 1932
Edward Kennedy, who was born on this date.

23 February 1821
John Keats, who died on this date.

24 February 1841
He was born in Liscannor, Co. Clare, on this date.

24 February 1981
The engagement of Prince Charles and Lady Diana Spencer.

25 February 1936
Ferdinand Porsche.

25 February 1958
The Campaign for Nuclear Disarmament, which was founded on this date.

25 February 1964
Mohammed Ali. Liston lost his title to Ali on this date.

26 February 1815
Napoleon was originally exiled to Elba, off the coast of Italy. He escaped on this date.

26 February 1839
The Grand National.

26 February 1991
Saddam Hussein of Iraq.

27 February 1902
John Steinbeck, who was born on this date.

27 February 1932
Elizabeth Taylor, who was born on this date, married
Richard Burton twice.

28 February 1909
Linus Pauling, who was born on this date, won the Nobel
Prize for Chemistry in 1934 and the Nobel Prize for Peace
in 1962.

28 February 1986
Sweden.

29 February
A leap year.

29 February 1743
James Gandon, who was born on this date.

29 February 1960
Morocco.

MARCH

1 March 1810
Chopin, who was born on this date, was Polish.

1 March 1886
Glen Miller, who was born on this date.

1 March 1910
David Niven, who was born on this date.

1 March 1932
Charles Lindbergh, whose baby was kidnapped on this date.

1 March 1940
Vivien Leigh won the Best Actress award on this date for her role in *Gone with the Wind*.

1 March 1965
Roger Casement.

2 March 1793
Sam Houston, who was born on this date.

2 March 1969
The Concorde.

3 March 1847
Bell was born on this date in Scotland.

3 March 1853
Vincent van Gogh, who was born on this date.

3 March 1923
Luce launched *Time* on this date.

3 March 1961
Fatima Whitbread, who was born on this date, is a champion javelin thrower.

3 March 1977
Brian Faulkner, who died on this date.

3 March 1991
Queen Elizabeth. The incident happened on this date.

4 March 1678
Antonio Vivaldi, who was born on this date.

4 March 1975
Charlie Chaplin, who received his knighthood on this date.

5 March 1953
Josef Stalin, who died on this date.

5 March 1966
Nelson's Pillar in O'Connell Street was blown up on this date.

6 March 1475
Michelangelo Buonarotti, who was born on this date.

6 March 1836
They were killed at the Alamo on this date.

6 March 1911
Ronald Reagan.

6 March 1944
Kiri Te Kanawa, who was born on this date, is from New Zealand.

6 March 1987
Near Zeebrugge, Belgium, on this date.

6 March 1988
In Gibraltar, on this date.

7 March 1876
The telephone was patented on this date by Alexander Graham Bell.

7 March 1960
Ivan Lendl, who was born on this date, never won the men's singles title.

8 March 1917
Count Ferdinand von Zeppelin.

9 March 1796
Napoleon Bonaparte.

10 March 1966
Frank O'Connor, who died on this date.

11 March 1931
Rupert Murdoch, who was born on this date, is a native of
Australia.

11 March 1952
The Hitch-Hiker's Guide to the Galaxy. Adams was born
on this date.

11 March 1955
Penicillin. Alexander Fleming died on this date.

11 March 1985
Mikhail Gorbachev.

12 March 1890
Nijinski, who was born on this date, was a ballet dancer.

12 March 1945
Anne Frank, who died in Belsen extermination camp on this
date, hid with her family in Amsterdam.

12 March 1946
Judy Garland was the mother of Liza Minelli, who was born
on this date.

13 March 1781
Uranus.

13 March 1960
Adam Clayton.

14 March 1879
In Germany, on this date.

14 March 1883
Karl Marx, who died on this date.

14 March 1933
Michael Caine, who was born on this date.

14 March 1991
The case of the Birmingham Six, who were released on this date.

15 March 44 BC
Julius Caesar was assassinated on this date.

16 March 1920
Leo McKern, who was born on this date, plays Rumpole of the Bailey.

16 March 1926
A liquid-fuel rocket.

16 March 1940
Bernardo Bertolucci, who was born on this date, is Italian.

16 March 1978
Aldo Moro, who was kidnapped on this date, was Italian.

17 March 1777
Prunty, who was born on this date, changed his name to Brontë.

17 March 1917
Tsar Nikolai (Nicholas) II gave up his throne on this date.

19 March 1906
Adolf Eichmann, who was born on this date, was hanged in Israel.

19 March 1932
The Sydney Harbour Bridge.

19 March 1936
Ursula Andress, who was born on this date, starred in *Doctor No*.

19 March 1950
Edgar Rice Burroughs.

20 March 1727
Isaac Newton, who died on this date.

20 March 1964
Brendan Behan, who died on this date.

20 March 1969
Yoko Ono.

21 March 1685
Johann Sebastian. He was born on this date.

21 March 1963
Alcatraz Prison, which closed on this date.

22 March 1903
Niagara Falls ran out of water on this date.

22 March 1913
Karl Malden, who was born on this date, starred in "The Streets of San Francisco".

22 March 1923
Marcel Marceau, who was born on this date.

22 March 1933
Dachau, which opened on this date, is just outside Munich.

23 March 1981
Ronald Biggs, who was apprehended in Barbados on this date. He had to be returned to Brazil and let free because he was the father of a Brazilian child.

23 March 1983
Barney Clarke, who died on this date, had an artificial heart, powered by a compressed-air machine in his hospital room.

24 March 1603
Anne Boleyn was the mother of Queen Elizabeth, who died on this date.

24 March 1905
Jules Verne, who died on this date.

24 March 1909
John Millington Synge, who died on this date.

24 March 1930
Steve McQueen, who was born on this date.

24 March 1953
King George V.

24 March 1976
Erwin Rommel was beaten by Montgomery, who died on this date.

24 March 1980
Archbishop Romero was killed in El Salvador, on this date.

24 March 1989
Off the coast of Alaska, on this date.

24 March 1991
Madonna, who won her Oscar on this date, sang "Sooner Or Later" in the film *Dick Tracy*.

25 March 1738
Ó Cearalláin, who died on this date, was blind.

25 March 1908
Co. Kerry. David Lean was born on this date.

25 March 1914
Marlon Brando, who was born on this date.

25 March 1947
Elton John. He was born on this date.

25 March 1957
The Treaty of Rome was signed on this date.

26 March 1827
Beethoven, who died on this date, completed nine symphonies in his lifetime. Scholars have since put together Beethoven's 10th Symphony, based on analysis of the composer's notes.

26 March 1920
The Black and Tans.

26 March 1931
Leonard Nimoy, who was born on this date, played the role of Mr Spock.

26 March 1944
Diana Ross, who was born on this date, used to play with the Supremes.

26 March 1979
Jimmy Carter. The peace treaty was signed on this date.

27 March 1794
The US Navy, established on this date, was founded by Wexfordman Commodore John Barry.

27 March 1863
Henry Royce, who was born on this date. Rolls was financier and salesman.

27 March 1968
Yuri Gagarin, the first person in space, died on this date.

27 March 1977
In Tenerife, Canary Islands, on this date. A KLM jet, taking off in fog, hit a Pan-American jet on the ground.

28 March 1957
Yeats. Jack B. Yeats died on this date.

28 March 1969
Dwight D. Eisenhower, who died on this date.

28 March 1979
There was a radiation leak on this date.

29 March 1867
Alaska, purchased from Russia on this date.

29 March 1886
Coca Cola, known then as the Esteemed Brain Tonic and Intellectual Beverage.

29 March 1919
Einstein's Theory of Relativity was confirmed on this date.

30 March 1853
In the Netherlands, on this date.

30 March 1945
Eric Clapton, who was born on this date, had a son named Conor.

30 March 1981
Ronald Reagan was shot by Hinckley on this date.

31 March 1596
René Descartes, who was born on this date, was a native of France.

31 March 1855
Charlotte Brontë, who died on this date.

31 March 1889
The Eiffel Tower.

31 March 1935
Richard Chamberlain, who was born on this date, played the role of an English lord in "Shogun".

31 March 1980
Jesse Owens, who died on this date, won his medals in Berlin.

APRIL

1 April 1578
William Harvey, who discovered the circulation of blood on this date.

1 April 1915
Bismarck, who died on this date, played an important role in uniting Germany.

1 April 1939
The Spanish Civil War.

1 April 1984
Marvin Gaye died on this date. His father shot him during an argument.

2 April 1805
Hans Christian Andersen, who was born on this date.

2 April 1865
Gen. Ulysses Grant accepted Lee's surrender on this date.

2 April 1982
Great Britain fought Argentina. Argentina invaded the Falklands (Malvinas) on this date.

3 April 1783
Rip van Winkle. Washington Irving was born on this date.

3 April 1860
The Pony Express. The company began delivering mail on this date.

3 April 1882
Jesse James was killed, on this date, by gang member Bob Ford.

3 April 1924
Marlon Brando, who was born on this date.

3 April 1930
Helmut Kohl, who was born on this date.

3 April 1936
Hauptmann, who was executed in the electric chair on this date, was German.

3 April 1961
Eddie Murphy, who was born on this date.

3 April 1991
Graham Greene.

4 April 1949
The North Atlantic Treaty, establishing NATO, was signed on this date.

4 April 1968
Memphis, where Martin Luther King was killed on this date, is in Tennessee.

4 April 1981 (a)
Bob Champion defeated cancer before winning the Grand National on Alderniti on this date.

4 April 1981 (b)
In Dublin, the year after Johnny Logan's first win.

5 April 1964
MacArthur, who died on this date, liberated the Philippines.

6 April 1874
Harry Houdini, who died on this date.

6 April 1896
The modern Olympic Games.

6 April 1909
Robert Peary, who reached the North Pole on this date, was American.

6 April 1917
The United States entered the First World War on this date.

6 April 1926
Ian Paisley, who was born on this date.

7 April 1739
Dick Turpin.

7 April 1891
Lego. Christiansen was born on this date.

7 April 1947
Henry Ford, who died on this date.

7 April 1968
Jim Clark, who was killed on this date, was a motor racing driver.

7 April 1973
Archbishop McQuaid, who died on this date, was Archbishop of Dublin.

8 April 1893
Mary Pickford, who was born on this date, was an actress.

8 April 1963
Julian Lennon, who was born on this date, is the son of John Lennon.

8 April 1973
Picasso, who died on this date, spent most of his life in France.

8 April 1986
Clint Eastwood.

9 April 1959
Frank Lloyd Wright, who died on this date.

9 April 1961
Albania.

9 April 1981
Bobby Sands won the Fermanagh-South Tyrone by-election on this date.

10 April 1989
Nick Faldo, who won the US Masters golf tournament on this date.

11 April 1929
Popeye first appeared in an American newspaper on this date.

12 April 1861
The Confederates attacked Fort Sumter in South Carolina on this date.

12 April 1928 (a)
The *Irish Times*. (See the answer to the next question.)

12 April 1928 (b)
Fitzmaurice took part in the first successful east-to-west flight across the Atlantic in the German plane *Bremen*, setting out from Baldonnell, Co. Dublin, on this date. The other pilots were Capt. Köhl and Baron von Hünefeld.

12 April 1941
Bobby Moore, who was born on this date, captained the English team in 1966.

12 April 1945
John F. Kennedy.

12 April 1954
"Rock Around the Clock" was recorded on this date. It featured in the film *Blackboard Jungle*.

12 April 1961
Soviet cosmonaut Yuri Gagarin, who was launched into space on this date.

12 April 1981 (a)
The first space shuttle, *Columbia* was launched into space. Unlike rockets and earlier spacecraft, the space shuttle is reusable.

12 April 1981 (b)
Joe Louis, who died on this date.

13 April 1742
In Dublin, in Fishamble Street, near Christ Church Cathedral, on this date.

13 April 1743
Thomas Jefferson.

13 April 1829
The Catholic Relief Act, removing formal discrimination against Catholics.

13 April 1906
Samuel Beckett, who was born on this date.

13 April 1980
He was 23.

14 April 1527
Philipstown, after King Felipe (Philip) II of Spain, who was married to Queen Mary of England.

14 April 1865
In the Ford Theatre, Washington, while watching *My American Cousin* on this date. He died the following day.

14 April 1912
The one that struck and sank the *Titanic* on this date.

15 April 1955
McDonald's.

15 April 1986
Tripoli, capital of Libya, was bombed on this date.

15 April 1989
Hillsboro Stadium, where ninety-five soccer fans were killed on this date, is in Sheffield.

16 April 1850
Marie Tussaud, who died on this date, founded Madame Tussaud's.

16 April 1867
Wilbur Wright, who was born on this date, was four years older than Orville.

16 April 1889
Charlie Chaplin, who was born on this date, was making fun of Adolf Hitler.

17 April 1790
Benjamin Franklin, who died on this date.

17 April 1970
The *Apollo 13* mission splashed down successfully on this date.

18 April 1775
Paul Revere. He made his famous journey on the night of 18/19 April.

18 April 1906
San Francisco.

19 April 1882
Charles Darwin, who died on this date.

19 April 1956
Grace Kelly, who married Prince Rainier of Monaco on this date.

19 April 1993
At Waco, Texas, on this date.

20 April 1889
Adolf Hitler, who was born in Austria on this date.

20 April 1912
Bram Stoker, who died on this date.

20 April 1941
Ryan O'Neill, who was born on this date.

20 April 1955
Einstein, who died on this date, lived in Germany and Switzerland.

21 April 1816
Charlotte Brontë, who was born on this date.

21 April 1910
Mark Twain, who died on this date.

21 April 1918
Baron von Richtofen, who was shot down and killed on this date, was better known as the Red Baron. Various First World War veterans have claimed the glory of shooting down the Baron.

22 April 1870
V. I. Lenin, born on this date, after whom it was named Leningrad.

22 April 1904
Oppenheimer, who was born on this date, was in charge of the project to make America's atomic bomb, code-named the Manhattan Project.

22 April 1926
Queen Elizabeth II, who was born on this date, has one sister, Margaret.

22 April 1933
Charles Rolls died first, on 12 July 1910. Henry Royce died on 22 April 1933.

23 April 1616
Shakespeare and Cervantes both died on this date.

24 April 1731
Daniel Defoe, who died on this date.

24 April 1916
Patrick Pearse. The Easter Rising began on this date.

24 April 1934
Warren Beatty is a brother of Shirley MacLaine, who was born on this date.

24 April 1981
A mail train. He returned to Brazil on this date, after extradition proceedings against him failed.

24 April 1986
Wallis Simpson, who died on this date, was the widow of the Duke of Windsor, formerly King Edward VIII.

25 April 1599
Oliver Cromwell, who was born on this date.

25 April 1719
Robinson Crusoe.

25 April 1874
Guglielmo Marconi, who was born on this date.

25 April 1939
Yes. Al Pacino, who was born on this date, won the Best Actor award in 1993 for his role in *The Scent of a Woman*.

25 April 1990
The Hubble Space Telescope was launched on this date in the space shuttle *Discovery*.

26 April 1452
Leonardo da Vinci, who was born on this date.

26 April 1894
Hess, who was born on this date, flew to Britain during the Second World War.

26 April 1937
The Spanish Civil War.

26 April 1986
Chernobyl is in Ukraine, but most of the radioactive fall-out from the accident has affected neighbouring Belarus.

26 April 1989
Lucille Ball, who died on this date.

27 April 1521
The Philippines, on the island of Mactan, where he was killed on this date.

27 April 1791
Samuel Morse, who was born on this date.

27 April 1827
Ulysses S. Grant, who was born on this date, was an American.

27 April 1937
The Golden Gate Bridge, which was opened on this date.

27 April 1953
Maud Gonne, who died on this date, was loved by William Butler Yeats.

28 April 1770
Sydney. Capt. James Cook landed in Botany Bay on this date.

28 April 1789 (a)
Fletcher Christian led the mutiny on the *Bounty*, which occurred on this date.

28 April 1789 (b)
The captain of the *Bounty* was Capt. William Bligh.

28 April 1945
Benito Mussolini, who died on this date.

28 April 1980
Alfred Hitchcock.

29 April 1769
Arthur Wellesley, the Duke of Wellington, who was born on this date.

29 April 1889
Because he had the same birthday as the Duke of Wellington.

29 April 1938
Ray McSharry, who was born on this date, was responsible for Agriculture.

29 April 1945
Eva Braun married Adolf Hitler on this date. They both committed suicide the following day.

30 April 1789
Washington was sworn in on this date in New York.

30 April 1945
Adolf Hitler, who died on this date.

MAY

1 May 1854
William Percy French, who was born on this date.

1 May 1931
The Empire State Building, which was officially opened on this date.

1 May 1945
Goebbels, who died with his family on this date.

1 May 1960
Paul Hewson, better known as Bono, was born on this date.

1 May 1967
Priscilla Beaulieu married Elvis Presley on this date.

1 May 1968
Legoland, which opened on this date, is in Denmark.

2 May 1519
Leonardo da Vinci, who died on this date.

2 May 1856
Matt Talbot.

2 May 1892
Baron von Richtofen, the Red Baron, was born on this date.

2 May 1904
"White Christmas". Bing Crosby was born on this date.

2 May 1923
Patrick Hillery, who was born on this date.

2 May 1969
The *Queen Elizabeth 2*.

2 May 1972
The Federal Bureau of Investigation (FBI).

2 May 1982
Argentina.

3 May 1916
Patrick Pearse.

4 May 1852
Lewis Carroll (pen name of Charles Lutwidge Dodgson).
Alice Liddell was born on this date.

4 May 1873
David Livingstone, who died on this date.

4 May 1929
Audrey Hepburn, who was born on this date.

4 May 1979
Margaret Thatcher, following a general election on this date.

4 May 1980
Yugoslavia. President Tito died on this date.

5 May 1821
Napoleon died on the South Atlantic island of St Helena on this date.

5 May 1943
The Monty Python team. Michael Palin was born on this date.

5 May 1961
Alan Shepard, who made the space trip on this date.

5 May 1981
Bobby Sands, who died on this date, began his fast on 1 March.

6 May 1626
The Dutch "bought" Manhattan on this date.

6 May 1840
The first adhesive postage stamp. It was issued by Britain, and, because it was their idea, they do not publish the name of the country on their stamps.

6 May 1856
Freud, who was born on this date, died in Britain, having fled there to escape Nazi persecution.

6 May 1882
Cavendish and Burke were killed in the Phoenix Park on this date.

171

6 May 1895
Rudolf Valentino was born in Italy on this date.

6 May 1910
King Edward VII, who died on this date, was the son of Queen Victoria.

6 May 1915
Orson Welles.

6 May 1937
The *Hindenburg*.

6 May 1954
Oxford.

6 May 1983
The forged diaries were supposed to be Adolf Hitler's. The German government exposed them as forgeries on this date.

7 May 1823
The 9th. Beethoven died on this date.

7 May 1840
Pyotr Ilyich Tchaikovsky, who was born on this date.

7 May 1901
High Noon. Gary Cooper was born on this date.

7 May 1915
The *Lusitania*, which was sunk on this date.

7 May 1936
Tony O'Reilly, who was born on this date.

7 May 1945
The Germans surrendered first, on 7 May 1945. The Japanese surrender did not come until the following September.

8 May 1828
Henri Dunant, who was born on this date, founded the Red Cross.

8 May 1884
Harry Truman, who was born on this date.

8 May 1902
Martinique is in the Caribbean Sea. Mount Pelee erupted on this date.

8 May 1940
Jaws. Peter Benchley was born on this date.

8 May 1945
This was VE (Victory in Europe) Day. People took the day off to celebrate the end of the war.

9 May 1860
Peter Pan. J. M. Barrie was born on this date.

9 May 1926
Richard Byrd.

10 May 1838
John Wilkes Booth, who was born on this date, shot Abraham Lincoln.

10 May 1863
Jackson, who died on this date, was a Confederate general.

10 May 1869
Two trains met at Promontory Point on this date, completing the rail link form the Atlantic to the Pacific. The celebrated Golden Spike, hammered in as the final link, was removed shortly after the event, because everybody knew it would be stolen.

10 May 1899
Fred Astaire, who was born on this date, and Ginger Rogers were dancers.

10 May 1904
Henry Morton Stanley, who died on this date, said these words to Dr Livingstone in Africa.

10 May 1940
Winston Churchill became Prime Minister of Great Britain on this date.

10 May 1960
Bono's real name is Paul Hewson, who was born on this date.

11 May 1904
Salvador Dali, who was born on this date, and Picasso were both Spanish.

11 May 1971
Seán Lemass.

11 May 1981
Bob Marley, who died on this date, was famous for his reggae music.

11 May 1985
Bradford. The tragedy happened on this date.

11 May 1988
It was Irving Berlin's 100th birthday.

12 May 1820
Florence Nightingale, who was born on this date.

12 May 1932
Bruno Hauptmann kidnapped the baby son of Charles Lindbergh. The child was found dead on this date.

13 May 1842
Sir Arthur Sullivan, who was born on this date.

13 May 1954
Johnny Logan.

13 May 1981
Pope John Paul survived an assassination attempt, which happened on this date.

14 May 1948
Israel.

15 May 1847
Daniel O'Connell, who died on this date.

15 May 1953
Mike Oldfield, who was born on this date.

15 May 1993 (a)
Niamh Kavanagh won the Eurovision Song Contest on this date in Millstreet, Co. Cork.

15 May 1993 (b)
Niamh Kavanagh's song was "In Your Eyes".

16 May 1905
Henry Fonda, who was born on this date.

16 May 1919
Liberace, who was born on this date, played the piano.

16 May 1955
Olga Korbut, who was born on this date, won her Olympic medals in Munich in 1972.

17 May 1900
Iran. The Ayatollah Khomeini was born on this date.

17 May 1969
His arms. McLean was the first person to row across the Atlantic, and he arrived in Co. Mayo on this date.

18 May 1804
Napoleon crowned himself Emperor of France on this date.

18 May 1868
The Tsar, who was born on this date, married Princess Alexandra of Hesse.

18 May 1919
Margot Fonteyn, who was born on this date, danced with Rudolf Nureyev.

18 May 1920
Pope John Paul II, who was born on this date.

18 May 1980
Mount St Helens.

19 May 1536
Anne Boleyn was the first. She was beheaded on this date.

19 May 1926
Malcolm X, who was born on this date.

19 May 1935
T. E. Lawrence (Lawrence of Arabia), who later died after a motorbike accident on this date.

20 May 1506
Christopher Columbus, who died on this date.

20 May 1932
Amelia Earhart, who arrived outside Derry on this date.

21 May 1927
He landed in Paris on this date.

21 May 1944
Bourke is the maiden name of President Robinson, who was born on this date.

21 May 1991
Rajiv Gandhi was assassinated on this date.

22 May 1859
Arthur Conan Doyle, who was born on this date.

22 May 1885
Victor Hugo, who died on this date.

22 May 1907
Laurence Olivier, who was born on this date.

22 May 1932
Lady Gregory, who died on this date, founded the Abbey Theatre with William Butler Yeats.

22 May 1946
George Best, who was born on this date.

22 May 1981
Peter Sutcliffe, who was sentenced on this date.

23 May 1498
Vasco da Gama reached India by sea on this date.

23 May 1701
Captain Kidd, who was hanged on this date, was a pirate.

23 May 1933
Joan, who was born on this date, and Jackie's surname is Collins.

23 May 1934
Bonnie Parker and Clyde Barrow (Bonnie and Clyde).

23 May 1945
In Nürnberg. Himmler committed suicide on this date.

24 May 1809
Dartmoor Prison, which was opened on this date.

24 May 1819
In 1901.

24 May 1844
Its inventor, Samuel Morse, on this date.

24 May 1883
The Brooklyn Bridge.

24 May 1928
William Trevor (pen name of Trevor Cox) was born on this date in Mitchelstown, Co. Cork.

24 May 1941
Bob Dylan, who was born on this date.

25 May 1916
Henry Ford. What he actually said, on this date, was, "History is more or less bunk."

25 May 1986
The Sport Aid run on this date was to raise funds for Africa.

26 May 1886
The Jazz Singer. Jolson was born on this date

26 May 1907
John Wayne, who was born on this date.

26 May 1988
Cats.

27 May 1703
St Petersburg, proclaimed capital city of Russia on this date.

27 May 1940
Dunkerque. The evacuation began on this date.

28 May 1968
Kylie Minogue, who was born on this date.

28 May 1972
King Edward VIII, who died on this date.

28 May 1987
In Red Square, Moscow, on this date.

28 May 1990
The Netherlands. The Australian tourists were killed by the IRA on this date.

29 May 1453
Istanbul (Constantinople) fell to the Turks on this date.

29 May 1911
W. S. Gilbert died on this date while rescuing a woman from drowning.

29 May 1914
The *Empress of Ireland* sank on the St Lawrence River on this date.

29 May 1953
Edmund Hillary and Tensing climbed Mount Everest on this date.

29 May 1985
The Heysel Stadium, where the disaster happened on this date, is in Belgium.

30 May 1536
Henry VIII married Jane Seymour on this date.

30 May 1911
The Indianapolis 500, which was first held on this date.

30 May 1912
He was killed in a plane crash on this date.

30 May 1959
Christopher Cockerell launched the first hovercraft on this date.

30 May 1960
Dr Zhivago. Boris Pasternak died on this date.

30 May 1973
Mary Robinson. Agreement among the political parties made it legal for Presidents Ó Dálaigh and Hillery to take office without an election.

31 May 1809
Haydn, who died on this date, was Austrian.

31 May 1837
Joe Grimaldi, who died on this date, was a clown.

31 May 1927
Fifteen million. The 15,007,003rd Model T Ford rolled off the assembly line on this date.

31 May 1930
Clint Eastwood, who was born on this date.

31 May 1965
He was the first non-American to win it.

JUNE

1 June 1762
Ignatius Rice, who was born on this date.

1 June 1910
Capt. Robert F. Scott, who set out from London on this date.

1 June 1926
Marilyn Monroe. She was born on this date.

1 June 1967
None. "Sergeant Pepper", which was released on this date, was their last album.

1 June 1968 (a)
Anne Sullivan taught Helen Keller, who died on this date.

1 June 1968 (b)
Jason Donovan, who was born on this date.

1 June 1971
Zimbabwe. This became Rhodesia's official name on this date.

2 June 1740
"Sadist". The Marquis de Sade, a deranged French writer, died on this date.

2 June 1896
Marconi patented his "wireless" on this date.

2 June 1953
In Westminster Abbey, on this date.

2 June 1954
He was elected Taoiseach.

2 June 1987
An Australian dingo or wild dog. Lindy Chamberlain
received a full pardon on this date, having spent time in jail
after being found guilty earlier of murdering her baby.

2 June 1990
Rex Harrison, who died on this date.

3 June 1899
Johann Strauss the Younger, who died on this date.

3 June 1946
Bikini. It was first shown in Paris on this date.

3 June 1963
Pope John XXIII.

3 June 1965
He walked in space from a Gemini spacecraft on this date.

4 June 1941
Kaiser Wilhelm II, who died on this date.

4 June 1944
Rome was liberated on this date. Paris was not liberated
until 25 August 1944.

4 June 1989 (a)
Russia. The accident happened on this date.

4 June 1989 (b)
Beijing, China. The massacre took place on this date.

5 June 1783
The Montgolfier brothers. They launched their balloon on
this date, but never actually took a balloon trip themselves.

5 June 1868
Cowgate, where James Connolly was born on this date, is
on the outskirts of Edinburgh.

5 June 1916
The Boer War. Kitchener died at sea during the First World War on this date.

5 June 1920
The Longest Day. Cornelius Ryan was born on this date.

5 June 1967
Israel. The war began on this date.

6 June 1944
Beaches in Normandy. The Normandy invasion took place on this date.

6 June 1949
Nineteen Eighty-Four. It was published on this date.

6 June 1968
Robert Kennedy, who died on this date, having been shot the previous evening in a Los Angeles hotel.

6 June 1976
Oil. Getty died on this date.

7 June 1329
Robert Bruce, who died on this date.

7 June 1905
Norway, which declared its independence from Sweden on this date.

7 June 1909
Jessica Tandy, who was born on this date.

7 June 1982
Elvis Presley. Graceland was first opened to the public on this date.

8 June 1986
Austria. Waldheim became president on this date but was
shunned by the international community because of his
involvement with the Nazis during the Second World War.

9 June 1870
Charles Dickens, who died on this date.

9 June 1898
Britain took a 99-year lease on Hong Kong on this date.

9 June 1934
Donald Duck. *The Wise Little Hen* was released on this
date.

10 June 1967
Israel won the war, which ended on this date.

10 June 1991
In the Philippines.

11 June 1509
Catherine of Aragón, daughter of Queen Isabella of Spain.
They were married on this date.

11 June 1955
At the Le Mans Grand Prix on this date.

12 June 1819
Charles Kingsley, who was born on this date.

12 June 1965
The Beatles.

12 June 1991
Boris Yeltsin. The election took place on this date.

13 June 1865
W. B. Yeats, who was born on this date, founded the Abbey
Theatre along with Lady Augusta Gregory.

13 June 1944
Germany. The first V1 rocket was dropped on London on this date.

14 June 1884
John McCormack was born in Athlone on this date.

14 June 1928
Guevara, who was born on this date, was killed in Bolivia.

14 June 1940
Paris.

14 June 1964
Nelson Mandela, who was sentenced on this date.

14 June 1968
Boris Becker. He won Wimbledon for the first time in 1985. Steffi Graf, who was born on this date, won Wimbledon for the first time in 1988.

15 June 1215
The Magna Carta was signed by King John on this date. It was a document showing laws that the King and Barons should be subject to.

15 June 1919
John Alcock and Arthur Brown crash-landed near Clifden, after becoming the first people to make a non-stop flight across the Atlantic.

16 June 1890
Stan Laurel.

16 June 1904
James Joyce.

16 June 1961
Rudolf Nureyev defected on this date.

16 June 1972
The Watergate. The whole affair, which led to the
resignation of President Nixon, became known as the
Watergate Affair. The burglary took place on this date.

17 June 1977
The National Aeronautics and Space Administration
(NASA) employed von Braun, who died on this date.

18 June 1815
Arthur Wellesley, the Duke of Wellington, on this date.

18 June 1928
Roald Amundsen was killed on this date.

18 June 1942
Wings. Paul McCartney was born on this date.

19 June 1937
J. M. Barrie, who died on this date.

19 June 1947
The Satanic Verses. Salman Rushdie was born on this
date.

20 June 1763
Wolfe Tone, who was born on this date, looked for help
from France.

20 June 1837
Queen Victoria, who became queen on this date.

21 June 1970
Soccer. The original World Cup was the Jules Rimet Cup,
and Brazil kept it after winning the competition for the third
time—on this date—in Mexico, defeating Italy.

22 June 1929
The stamp, issued on this date, marked the anniversary of
Catholic Emancipation.

22 June 1936
Kris Kristofferson, who was born on this date, is also a successful singer.

22 June 1949
Meryl Streep, who was born on this date.

23 June 1848
A patent for the saxophone was granted on this date.

23 June 1875
Isaac Singer, who died on this date, invented the sewing machine.

23 June 1985
The Air India plane, which crashed on this date, was en route from Canada.

24 June 1314
The Scots won the Battle of Bannockburn on this date.

24 June 1973
Éamon de Valera, whose second term expired on this date.

25 June 1876
Gen. George Custer. "Custer's Last Stand" took place on this date.

25 June 1964
Gay Byrne married Kathleen Watkins on this date.

26 June 1963
Kennedy, who made a famous speech in Berlin on this date, visited Ireland before returning to America.

26 June 1976
Pictures of Mars were beamed back on this date.

27 June 1846
Parnell's home, Avondale, is near Rathdrum, Co. Wicklow.
Parnell was born on this date.

28 June 1861
Australia. He died of starvation on this date, after
completing his journey only to find that the people at the
base camp had gone home, thinking that Burke and his
companions were dead in the wilderness.

28 June 1914
Archduke Franz Ferdinand and his wife were assassinated
in Sarajevo on this date.

28 June 1986
Richard Branson, who successfully completed the high-
speed crossing on this date.

29 June 1986
Argentina.

30 June 1894
Tower Bridge, officially opened on this date, crosses the
River Thames.

30 June 1936
Only one. *Gone with the Wind* was published on this date.

JULY

1 July 1681
St Oliver Plunkett, who was hanged on this date.

1 July 1863
The Battle of Gettysburg, which began on this date.

1 July 1916 (a)
The Coca Cola bottle was launched on this date.

1 July 1916 (b)
The Battle of the Somme, which began on this date.

1 July 1961
Carl Lewis, who was born on this date.

2 July 1865
The Salvation Army, which was established on this date.

2 July 1900
Count Ferdinand von Zeppelin.

2 July 1922
The Four Courts.

3 July 1987
During the Second World War. Barbie was sentenced to life imprisonment on this date.

3 July 1988
In the Persian Gulf on this date. The plane was mistaken for a fighter plane.

4 July 1776
The Americans declared their independence from England on this date.

4 July 1826
Both died on this date, which was the 50th anniversary of the Declaration of Independence.

4 July 1881
Billy the Kid, who died on this date.

4 July 1976
Uganda. The raid took place on this date.

5 July 1826
Singapore. Raffles died on this date.

5 July 1975
Arthur Ashe. He beat Connors on this date.

6 July 1535
St Thomas More, who was beheaded on this date.

6 July 1946
Sylvester Stallone, who was born on this date.

6 July 1971
Louis Armstrong, who died on this date.

7 July 1930
Sherlock Holmes. The author, Sir Arthur Conan Doyle, died on this date.

7 July 1982
Queen Elizabeth II. The incident happened on this date.

7 July 1985
Becker was 17 when he won his first Wimbledon title on this date.

7 July 1990
Martina Navratilova, who won her ninth title on this date.

8 July 1853
Japan.

8 July 1967
Vivien Leigh, who died on this date.

8 July 1978
Their climb, was the first to be made without the assistance of oxygen.

10 July 1834
Whistler's Mother. Whistler was born on this date.

10 July 1927
Kevin O'Higgins, who died on this date.

10 July 1985 (a)
In New Zealand, in the port of Auckland, on this date.

10 July 1985 (b)
France.

11 July 1690
In the Battle of the Boyne at Oldbridge, Co. Louth, on this date (not on the twelfth, as many people believe).

11 July 1915
Yul Brynner, who was born on this date.

12 July 1910
Charles Rolls, who died on this date.

12 July 1937
Bill Cosby, who was born on this date.

12 July 1949
Douglas Hyde, who died on this date

13 July 1942
Raiders of the Lost Ark. Harrison Ford was born on this date.

14 July 1789
François Mitterand. The storming of the Bastille prison on 14 July 1789 marked the beginning of the French Revolution.

15 July
This is St Swithin's Day. If it rains on this day, it will rain for the next forty days—give or take several days here and there.

15 July 1606
Rembrandt, who was born on this date.

15 July 1899
Seán Lemass, who was born on this date.

15 July 1904
Anton Chekhov, who died on this date.

15 July 1927
Constance Markievicz, who died on this date.

16 July 1945
The United States. No, not Japan: the Americans tested one bomb to be sure that it worked, at Alamogordo, New Mexico, on this date.

17 July 1938
"Wrong-Way" Corrigan landed on Portmarnock strand, Co. Dublin, on this date. The authorities would not give him permission to cross the Atlantic so he got permission to fly to California. The man said he made a mistake.

17 July 1951
The Abbey Theatre.

18 July 1877
Thomas Edison. He first tested his machine on this date.

18 July 1955
Walt Disney's Disneyland opened on this date.

19 July 1814
Samuel Colt, who was born on this date.

20 July 1944
Adolf Hitler. The attempt on his life took place on this date.

20 July 1982
The IRA. The bombing took place on this date.

21 July 1796
Robert Burns was 37 when he died on this date.

21 July 1899
Bullfighting. Hemingway was born on this date.

21 July 1928
The Field. John B. Keane was born on this date.

21 July 1969
The Sea of Tranquillity is on the Moon, and Armstrong first walked on the Moon on this date.

21 July 1976
Christopher Ewart-Biggs, who was assassinated on this date, was the British Ambassador to Ireland.

23 July 1693
Patrick Sarsfield, who died on this date.

23 July 1803
Robert Emmet. His ill-fated rising took place on this date.

23 July 1980
Peter Sellers, who died on this date.

23 July 1986
The wedding of Prince Andrew and Sarah Ferguson, which took place on this date.

24 July 1802
Alexandre Dumas, who was born on this date.

25 July 1554
They were Catholic, and were married on this date.

25 July 1909
Louis Blériot, who made the crossing from Calais to Dover on this date.

26 July 1856
George preferred to be called Bernard. He was born on this date.

27 July 1980
The Shah died in Egypt on this date.

28 July 1586
Sir Walter Raleigh. The potato is supposed to have reached Ireland on this date.

29 July 1890
Vincent van Gogh.

29 July 1948
London. The games opened on this date.

29 July 1955
"This Is Your Life".

29 July 1981
In St Paul's Cathedral on this date.

30 July 1863
Henry Ford, who was born on this date.

30 July 1930
In Montevideo, Uruguay, on this date.

30 July 1958
Lucozade. Daley Thompson was born on this date.

30 July 1966 (a)
In Wembley Stadium, London, on this date.

30 July 1966 (b)
Geoff Hurst scored a hat trick—three goals—during the World Cup final on this date.

31 July 1556
The Society of Jesus (Jesuits). Loyola died on this date.

31 July 1917
Francis Ledwidge, who died on this date.

31 July 1975
The Miami Showband. The ambush took place at Bessbrook, near Newry, on this date.

August

1 August 1779
"The Star-Spangled Banner", written by Francis Scott Key, who was born on this date.

1 August 1914
Germany declared war on Russia on this date.

2 August 1876
James "Wild Bill" Hickok. He was shot in the back by Jack McCall in Deadwood, South Dakota, on this date.

2 August 1990
Saddam Hussein. The invasion of Kuwait began on this date.

3 August 1492
Christopher Columbus. He set out for India on this date, but reached America instead.

3 August 1916
Roger Casement, who was hanged on this date.

4 August 1900
Queen Elizabeth II. Elizabeth Bowes-Lyon married the Duke of York, the future King George VI, in 1923.

4 August 1914
Britain declared war on Germany on this date.

5 August 1958
The *Nautilus* passed under the North Pole on this date.

5 August 1962
Marilyn Monroe (original name Norma Jean Baker), who died on this date.

5 August 1984
Richard Burton, who died on this date.

6 August 1775
Daniel O'Connell, who was born on this date.

6 August 1945
An atomic bomb, which destroyed the city of Hiroshima on this date.

6 August 1978
Giovanni Battista Montini, Pope Paul VI, who died on this date.

7 August 1903
Africa. Louis Leakey was born on this date.

8 August 1961
Dave Evans, who was born on this date and is better known as the Edge, is a member of U2.

8 August 1963
A train. The incident, known as the Great Train Robbery, happened when a night mail train was relieved of £2.5 million in used, and therefore untraceable, banknotes. Biggs was caught and jailed but escaped to Brazil.

8 August 1974
Richard Nixon, who announced his resignation on this date, to take effect the following day.

8 August 1991
John McCarthy is a journalist.

8 August 1992
Michael Carruth, who won his boxing gold medal on this date.

9 August 1945
Nagasaki, which was destroyed by an atomic bomb on this date.

9 August 1974
Gerald Ford, who was sworn in on this date.

10 August 1984
At the Los Angeles Olympic Games on this date.

12 August 1908
The Model T Ford.

13 August 1860
Annie Oakley, who was born on this date.

13 August 1899
In England, on this date.

13 August 1961
They began building a wall around their sector of Berlin on this date. This structure became the long-lasting Berlin Wall.

14 August 1961
Andrew Lloyd Weber. Sarah Brightman was born on this date.

14 August 1969
On the streets of Belfast and Derry, on this date.

15 August 1769
Wellington, born on 29 April 1769, was older than
Napoleon, who was born on 15 August 1769.

15 August 1771
Sir Walter Scott, who was born on this date.

15 August 1914
President Woodrow Wilson opened the Panama Canal on
this date.

16 August 1896
In Canada, on the Klondike River, where gold was
discovered on this date.

16 August 1958
Madonna, who was born on this date.

16 August 1977
Elvis Presley, who died on this date.

17 August 1920
Maureen O'Hara, who was born on this date.

17 August 1987
Berlin. Hess died on this date.

19 August 1871
The Wright Brothers. Orville Wright was born on this date.

19 August 1887
Francis Ledwidge, who was born on this date.

19 August 1977
Julius Marx—better known as Groucho—was a comic
actor, the oldest of the Marx Brothers. He died on this
date.

19 August 1987
He killed a total of fourteen people on this date with his small arsenal of guns, including his mother, then shot himself when cornered.

19 August 1991
Cable News Network.

20 August 1940
In Mexico, on this date.

21 August 1930
Prince Margaret, who was born on this date, is younger than Queen Elizabeth. If she was older she would be the Queen.

21 August 1959
It means "fifty", and refers to the fact that Hawaii is the fiftieth state of the United States. It became the fiftieth state on this date.

22 August 1911
The *Mona Lisa*.

22 August 1922
At Béal na mBlátha, near Macroom, on this date.

22 August 1957
Steve Davis, who was born on this date.

23 August 1926
Rudolf Valentino.

24 August 79
Vesuvius (modern Monte Vesuvio).

24 August 1990
Brian Keenan, the Beirut hostage who was released on this date.

25 August 1875
The English Channel. Webb accomplished the swim on this date.

25 August 1882
Seán T. O'Kelly, who was born on this date.

25 August 1930
Indiana Jones and the Last Crusade. Connery, who was born on this date, played Indiana Jones's father.

25 August 1944
Paris was liberated on this date. The German commander, Gen. von Choltitz, gave himself up rather than carry out Hitler's orders to blow up bridges and buildings.

25 August 1954
Declan McManus, who was born on this date, is better known as Elvis Costello.

26 August 1819 (a)
Prince Albert, who was born on this date, was the father of the future King Edward VII.

26 August 1819 (b)
Prince Albert was married to Queen Victoria.

26 August 1959
The Mini, which was launched on this date.

26 August 1978
He was the Pope. Named John Paul I, he became Pope on this date.

27 August 1882 (a)
Sam Goldwyn, who was born on this date, was a film producer.

27 August 1882 (b)
MGM stands for Metro-Goldwyn-Meyer. (See the previous answer.)

27 August 1883
Krakatoa, which erupted on this date. About 36,000 people were killed, mainly because of the tidal waves that followed the eruption.

27 August 1908
Lyndon Johnson, who was born on this date.

27 August 1910
Mother Teresa, who was born on this date.

27 August 1957
Bernhard Langer, who was born on this date, is German.

27 August 1979
Lord Mountbatten, who was killed at Mullaghmore on this date.

28 August 1828
The invasion of Russia by France under Napoleon. Tolstoy was born on this date.

28 August 1988
James Joyce. Film director John Huston died on this date.

29 August 1871
Jack B. Yeats, who was born on this date, was younger than his brother William B. Yeats, who was born in 1865.

29 August 1877
The Church of Jesus Christ of Latter-Day Saints (Mormons). Brigham Young died on this date.

29 August 1949
Sommersby. Actor Richard Gere was born on this date.

29 August 1958
Lenny Henry and Michael Jackson were both born on this date.

29 August 1975
Éamon de Valera was 92 when he died on this date.

30 August 1870
Maria Montessori, who was born on this date, opened her first school in Italy.

31 August 1945
Van Morrison was born on this date in Belfast.

31 August 1986
Henry Moore's Yeats sculpture is in St Stephen's Green, Dublin. Moore died on this date.

SEPTEMBER

1 September 1715
King Louis XIV, who died on this date.

1 September 1939
Germany's invasion of Poland on this date.

1 September 1985
The *Titanic*. Ballard found the wreck on this date.

2 September 1666
London. The fire started on this date.

2 September 1937
The modern Olympic Games were founded by de Coubertin, who died on this date.

2 September 1945
The Japanese formally surrendered on this date.

2 September 1952
Jimmy Connors, who was born on this date, won the championship twice.

2 September 1973
J. R. R. Tolkien, who died on this date.

2 September 1980
Terry Fox was Canadian, and he abandoned his run on this date. His achievement is all the greater because he made the run while wearing an artificial leg.

3 September 1658
Oliver Cromwell.

3 September 1783
The American War of Independence. The Treaty of Paris, by which Britain recognised the existence of the United States, was signed on this date.

3 September 1939
Great Britain, France, New Zealand, and Australia.

3 September 1967
On the right: they changed from left to right on this date, to make their road system compatible with neighbouring countries. It was a huge undertaking: think of all the road markings that had to be changed at every junction, for example.

4 September 1886
Geronimo, who surrendered on this date.

4 September 1989
Insp. Maigret. Simenon died on this date.

5 September 1820
The Christian Brothers received papal recognition on this date.

5 September 1847
The Pony Express. Jesse James was born on this date.

5 September 1972
At the Olympic Games in Munich on this date.

5 September 1982
Douglas Bader, who died on this date, was a pilot with no legs, having lost them in an accident.

7 September 1981
Christy Brown, author of *My Left Foot*.

8 September 1504
Michelangelo Buonarotti, who unveiled his statue of David on this date.

8 September 1925
Peter Sellers, who was born on this date.

9 September 1976
Mao Zedong, who died on this date, aged 82.

9 September 1978
Martina Navratilova is a native of the Czech Republic (then Czechoslovakia). She defected on this date.

10 September 1898
Pierre and Marie Curie discovered radium on this date.

11 September 1649
Drogheda. The massacre of about 1,500 people took place on this date.

11 September 1917
Imelda Marcos. Ferdinand Marcos was born on this date.

11 September 1971
Nikita Khrushchev, who died on this date, ruled the Soviet Union after Stalin and before Brezhnev.

12 September 1953
Jacqueline Lee-Bouvier married John F. Kennedy on this date.

12 September 1977
Steve Biko, who died on this date, was South African.

13 September 1793
Hoban was from Co. Kilkenny. The cornerstone of the White House was laid on this date.

14 September 1916
Tanks were first used on this date during the Battle of the Somme.

14 September 1982
Princess Grace of Monaco, who died on this date.

15 September 1789
The Last of the Mohicans. The author was born on this date.

15 September 1890
Agatha Christie, who was born on this date.

16 September 1620
The *Mayflower*, which left Plymouth, England, on this date.

16 September 1945
John McCormack, who died on this date, was given the title of Count by the Pope.

17 September 1977
Maria Callas, who died on this date, was a singer.

18 September 1709
A lexicographer is a person who compiles dictionaries. Samuel Johnson was born on this date.

20 September 1519
Fernão de Magalhães (Ferdinand Magellan). His journey began at Sevilla, Spain, on this date.

20 September 1580
Sir Francis Drake, who was born on this date.

20 September 1803
Robert Emmet, who was hanged on this date.

20 September 1934
Sophia Loren was born in Rome on this date.

20 September 1957
Jean Sibelius, who died on this date, was Finnish.

20 September 1967
Queen Elizabeth 2.

21 September 1866
The War of the Worlds. H. G. Wells was born on this date.

21 September 1931 (a)
Larry Hagman, who was born on this date.

21 September 1931 (b)
John Ross. (See the previous answer.)

22 September 1980
The Iran-Iraq war began on this date.

23 September 1949
Bruce Springsteen, who was born on this date.

24 September 1786
Charles Bianconi, who was born on this date.

24 September 1942
Linda McCartney was born in the United States on this date.

25 September 1944
Douglas. Kirk is the father; Michael, who was born on this date, is the son.

25 September 1952
Christopher Reeve, who was born on this date, will be remembered for his role as Superman.

26 September 1888
Cats. T. S. Eliot was born on this date.

26 September 1948
Olivia Newton-John, who was born on this date.

28 September 1891
Herman Melville, who died on this date.

28 September 1895
Louis Pasteur, who died on this date.

28 September 1978
Albino Luciani, who died on this date, took the name of John Paul I.

29 September 1547
Don Quixote was the character created by Cervantes, who was born on this date.

29 September 1758
Adm. Horatio Nelson, who was born on this date.

29 September 1900
Constance Gore-Booth married Count Casimir Dunin-Markievicz on this date.

29 September 1935
Jerry Lee Lewis, who was born on this date.

29 September 1979
Pope John Paul, who arrived in Ireland on this date.

30 September 1900
Oscar Wilde, who died on this date.

30 September 1938
Chamberlain promised "Peace in our time" on this date—
less than a year before the outbreak of the Second World
War.

30 September 1955
James Dean, who was killed on this date.

OCTOBER

1 October 1917
Bishop Cahal Daly, who was born on this date.

1 October 1969
Concorde broke the sound barrier for the first time, on this
date, over France.

2 October 1909
The first match was played on this date at Twickenham,
Middlesex.

2 October 1985
Rock Hudson died of AIDS on this date.

3 October 1226
The Order of Friars Minor (Franciscans). Bernardone is
better known as St Francis of Assisi, and he died on this
date.

3 October 1975 (a)
The Netherlands.

3 October 1975 (b)
At Monasterevin, Co. Kildare.

3 October 1990
Helmut Kohl.

4 October 1895
Buster Keaton, who was born on this date.

4 October 1957 (a)
Sputnik. (See the next answer.)

4 October 1957 (b)
The Soviet Union launched the first satellite, *Sputnik*, on this date.

5 October 1954
Bob Geldof, who was born on this date.

5 October 1968
In Derry, on this date.

6 October 1891
Charles Stewart Parnell.

6 October 1914
Thor Heyerdahl, who was born on this date, is Norwegian.

6 October 1981
Tully stood close to the President of Egypt, Anwar al-Sadat, when he was assassinated on this date.

7 October 1919
KLM, established on this date.

7 October 1985
The *Achille Lauro*, which was hijacked on this date, is an Italian ship.

8 October 1871
Chicago was destroyed by the fire, which began on this date.

9 October 1776
San Francisco was established on this date by Franciscan missionaries.

9 October 1940
John Lennon, who was born on this date.

11 October 1809
Meriwether Lewis and William Clark were explorers of America. After the Louisiana Territory was purchased from France in 1803, President Jefferson sent the two men to lead a fact-finding expedition across the continent. Lewis died a few years later on this date.

12 October 1492
The Bahamas, on this date.

12 October 1975
Pope Paul VI.

12 October 1984 (a)
In Brighton, on this date.

12 October 1984 (b)
Margaret Thatcher.

13 October 1941
Paul Simon, who was born on this date, used to be in partnership with Art Garfunkel.

14 October 1066
Duke William of Normandy (William the Conqueror) won the Battle of Hastings on this date.

14 October 1882
Éamon de Valera, who was born on this date.

14 October 1890
Nixon was Vice-President under President Dwight D. Eisenhower, who was born on this date.

14 October 1940
Cliff Richard, who was born on this date.

14 October 1944
Rommel committed suicide on this date. The alternative was to be tried and executed for his part in the attempt on Hitler's life.

14 October 1947
The sound barrier. Chuck Yeager was the first person to travel faster than sound, which he did on this date.

14 October 1977
Bing Crosby was playing golf in Spain when he died on this date.

15 October 1881
P. G. Wodehouse, who was born on this date, created Jeeves.

16 October 1793
Marie-Antoinette, who was guillotined on this date.

16 October 1815
To St Helena, on this date.

16 October 1925 (a)
Angela Lansbury, who was born on this date.

16 October 1925 (b)
Jessica Fletcher. (See the previous question.)

16 October 1854
Oscar Wilde was born in Westland Row, Dublin, on this date.

16 October 1886
Israel. David Ben-Gurion was born on this date.

16 October 1890
The Anglo-Irish Treaty, which partitioned Ireland. Collins was born on this date.

16 October 1978
In the Sistine Chapel. The cardinals elected Karol Wojtyla on this date.

17 October 1849
Frédéric Chopin, who died on this date, composed for the piano.

17 October 1931
Income tax evasion. Capone was found guilty on this date, and sentenced to eleven years in jail.

17 October 1973
The Arab states began using oil as a weapon on this date. They increased the price by 70 per cent and cut back on production, thus making huge difficulties for western economies.

17 October 1979
Calcutta. It was announced on this date that she was to receive the Nobel Prize for Peace.

18 October 1931
Thomas Edison, who died on this date, was quite deaf.

18 October 1956
Martina Navratilova, who was born on this date, has won the title nine times.

18 October 1989
San Francisco.

19 October 1745
Jonathan Swift, who formerly appeared on the £10 note, died on this date.

19 October 1781
George Washington accepted Cornwallis's surrender on this date.

19 October 1931
John Le Carré, who was born on this date.

21 October 1805
Adm. Horatio Nelson won the Battle of Trafalgar on this date, and was himself killed.

21 October 1833
Alfred Nobel, who was born on this date, made his fortune from dynamite.

21 October 1904
Patrick Kavanagh, who was born on this date.

21 October 1917
Dizzie Gillespie, who was born on this date, played the trumpet.

21 October 1956
Star Wars. Carrie Fisher was born on this date.

21 October 1966
Aberfan, where the disaster happened on this date, is in Wales.

21 October 1973
Queen Elizabeth officially opened the Sydney Opera House on this date.

22 October 1811
Liszt, who was born on this date, was Hungarian.

23 October 1921
The pneumatic or air-filled tyre. The principle had been
patented in 1845, but Dunlop, who died on this date, hit on
the idea himself and he went into business making his
tyres.

23 October 1940
Pelé (nickname of Edson do Nascimento), who was born on
this date.

23 October 1987
Lester Piggot, who was sent to jail on this date.

24 October 1929
The Wall Street Crash began on this date. (See the related
answer for 29 October.)

24 October 1936
Bill Wyman, who was born on this date, is a member of the
Rolling Stones.

25 October 1825
Johann Strauss, who was born on this date.

25 October 1854
The Charge of the Light Brigade, a brave but pointless
manoeuvre on this date by the British against the
Russians, which left 247 dead or wounded.

25 October 1960
Agricultural tractors. Ferguson died on this date.

26 October 1881 (b)
The gunfight took place at the OK Corral on this date, in
Tombstone, Arizona.

26 October 1881 (b)
Doc Holliday was a dentist. (See the previous answer.)

27 October 1939
John Cleese, who was born on this date.

27 October 1971
Zaïre, which took its new name on this date, used to be the Belgian Congo.

27 October 1978
Israel. Prime Minister Menachem Begin shared the prize with Sadat.

28 October 1886
The Statue of Liberty, which was inaugurated on this date.

28 October 1958
Twenty-two. Cardinal Roncalli became Pope on this date as John XXIII.

29 October 1618
Sir Walter Raleigh, who was beheaded on this date.

29 October 1897
Goebbels, who was born on this date.

29 October 1929
New York Stock Exchange (the Wall Street market) finally crashed on this date.

29 October 1949
Jaws. Richard Dreyfuss was born on this date.

30 October 1926
Harry Houdini (stage name of Ehrich Weiss), who died on this date.

30 October 1932
Candice Bergen. Louis Malle was born on this date.

30 October 1938
The "Invasion from Mars" programme was broadcast in America on this date.

30 October 1979
The "bouncing bomb", which skipped over the water like a flat stone, bypassing German defences at dams. Wallis died on this date.

30 October 1984
Indira Gandhi was assassinated on this date.

31 October 1517
Martin Luther, who nailed his theses to the church door on this date.

31 October 1795
John Keats, who was born on this date.

31 October 1961
Larry Mullen, who was born on this date.

31 October 1971
The Post Office Tower in London was badly damaged on this date.

NOVEMBER

1 November 1625
Oliver Plunkett, who was born on this date, was Archbishop of Armagh.

1 November 1884
The GAA was founded in Hayes's Hotel, Thurles, on this date.

1 November 1920
Kevin Barry, who was hanged on this date.

1 November 1976
Jimmy Carter, who was elected US President on this date, was a Democrat.

1 November 1988
Batman's sidekick, Robin, was killed in the *Batman* comic of this date.

2 November 1734
Daniel Boone, who was born on this date.

2 November 1913
Burt Lancaster, who was born on this date.

2 November 1950
George Bernard Shaw, who died on this date.

3 November 1871
Henry Morton Stanley and Dr David Livingstone. Stanley found Livingstone on this date.

3 November 1921
Charles Bronson, who was born on this date.

3 November 1923
Cardinal Ó Fiaich, who was born on this date, came from Crossmaglen.

3 November 1957
Laika was the first animal in space. The dog was launched on this date, but died in space because there was no system for returning it to earth.

4 November 1884
Sir Harry Ferguson, who was born on this date, built and flew his own plane in 1909.

4 November 1979
Staff in the US embassy in Tehran were taken hostage on this date.

4 November 1980
Ronald Reagan, who was elected on this date.

4 November 1985
Éamonn Andrews, who died on this date.

5 November 1605
Guy Fawkes was caught trying to blow up the Houses of Parliament in London on this date.

5 November 1991
Robert Maxwell, who died on this date.

5 November 1913
Scarlett O'Hara in *Gone with the Wind*. Vivien Leigh was born on this date.

7 November 1975
Dr Tiede Herrema, who was released on this date.

8 November 1656
Halley's Comet. Halley was born on this date.

8 November 1900
Margaret Mitchell, who was born on this date, lived in Atlanta.

8 November 1922
Barnard, who was born on this date, performed his first heart transplant in South Africa.

8 November 1987
In Enniskillen. The bombing happened on this date.

9 November 1875
Sir Hugh Lane, who was born on this date.

9 November 1922
The SS, which was formed on this date.

9 November 1926
Jack Keyes-Byrne, who was born on this date, is better known as Hugh Leonard.

9 November 1938
The German Jewish community, which was terrorised on this date.

9 November 1970
Charles de Gaulle died on this date.

10 November 1879
Patrick Pearse, who was born on this date, had a squint, which would not be noticed from a side view.

10 November 1925
Richard Burton was born on this date in Wales.

10 November 1982
Two: Yuri Andropov and Konstantin Chernenko. Brezhnev died on this date.

11 November 1918
The First World War ended on this date.

11 November 1940
The Willys GP (general-purpose) vehicle, which was introduced on this date, became known as the "Jeep".

12 November 1961
Nadia Comanech, who was born on this date.

13 November 1985
In Colombia. Nevado del Ruíz erupted on this date.

13 November 1987
Menten, who died on this date, had his Irish home in Co. Waterford.

14 November 1180
St Lorcán Ó Tuathail, who died on this date, was bishop of Dublin.

14 November 1948
Prince Charles, the eldest son of Queen Elizabeth II, was born on this date. At the time of his birth his mother, then Princess Elizabeth, was first in line for the throne.

15 November 1864
Sherman destroyed Atlanta on this date.

15 November 1891
Erwin Rommel, who was born on this date.

15 November 1956
Elvis Presley. The film had its première in New York on this date.

15 November 1985
Garret FitzGerald. The Anglo-Irish Agreement was signed on this date.

16 November 1960
Clark Gable, who died on this date.

16 November 1961
Frank Bruno, who was born on this date.

17 November 1869
France. The Suez Canal opened on this date.

17 November 1974
Erskine Childers, who died on this date.

18 November 1626
St Peter's Basilica was consecrated on this date.

18 November 1987
There was a serious fire in the station on this date.

18 November 1991
Terry Waite, who was released on this date along with American Thomas Sutherland.

19 November 1798
Theobald Wolfe Tone, who died on this date.

19 November 1863
The Gettysburg Address, made by Lincoln on this date.

19 November 1977
Anwar al-Sadat, who visited Israel on this date.

20 November 1945
In Nürnberg. The trials began on this date.

20 November 1947
Queen Victoria. Philip and Elizabeth were married on this date.

20 November 1975
Gen. Francisco Franco, who died on this date.

21 November 1974
Six. The Birmingham pub bombs exploded on this date, killing twenty-one people.

22 November 1718
Edward Teach, who died on this date, was better known as Blackbeard.

22 November 1913
Benjamin Britten, who was born on this date, was a British composer.

22 November 1943
Billie Jean King, who was born on this date, was a tennis champion.

22 November 1946
The Biro ballpoint pen went on sale in England on this date.
It had been in use with military personnel during the
Second World War.

22 November 1963
In Dallas, Texas, on this date.

22 November 1967
Boris Becker was born on this date.

22 November 1991
Margaret Thatcher resigned as Prime Minister on this date.

23 November 1852
Pillar boxes were introduced on this date.

23 November 1859
Billy the Kid, who was born on this date.

24 November 1859
Charles Darwin. *On the Origin of Species by Means of
Natural Selection* was published on this date.

24 November 1952
Kaliber. Billy Connolly was born on this date.

24 November 1963
Jack Ruby shot Lee Harvey Oswald, Kennedy's alleged
assassin, on this date.

24 November 1991
Freddie Mercury, who died on this date, was the lead singer
with Queen.

25 November 1835
Carnegie, who was born on this date, made most of his
money from steel.

25 November 1844
Karl Benz.

25 November 1914
Marilyn Monroe married Joe Di Maggio, who was born on this date.

25 November 1952
The Mousetrap.

25 November 1974
The United Nations. U Thant died on this date.

25 November 1984
"Do They Know It's Christmas?", which was recorded on this date.

26 November 1910
Cyril Cusack, who was born on this date.

26 November 1922 (a)
Charles Schulz, who was born on this date, created "Peanuts." Charlie Brown, Snoopy and company.

26 November 1922 (b)
Tutankhamun's tomb, which was found on this date, was intact. Other pharaohs' tombs had been ravaged by grave-robbers over the centuries.

26 November 1939
Tina Turner, who was born on this date.

27 November 1921
Dubcek, who was born on this date, was Prime Minister of Czechoslovakia.

30 November 1667
Jonathan Swift, who was born on this date, had his portrait on the former £10 note.

30 November 1835
Mark Twain, who was born on this date.

30 November 1874
Winston Churchill, who was born on this date.

30 November 1929
Richard Byrd, who made the flight on this date.

30 November 1967
Co. Monaghan.

DECEMBER

1 December 1935
Woody Allen (stage name of Allen Konigsberg), who was born on this date.

1 December 1939
Lee Trevino, who was born on this date, was a champion golfer.

1 December 1989
Mikhail Gorbachev. He met Pope John Paul II on this date.

1 December 1990
They were standing in the Channel Tunnel. The first contact between the two ends of the tunnel was made on this date.

2 December 1697
St Paul's Cathedral, which was opened on this date.

2 December 1804
Napoleon Bonaparte. He crowned himself on this date.

2 December 1859
John Brown, who was hanged on this date, was an anti-slavery campaigner.

2 December 1982
An artificial heart. Barney Clark underwent the operation on this date.

3 December 1552
Nagasaki. Francis Xavier died on this date.

3 December 1894
Robert Louis Stevenson, who died on this date.

3 December 1967
South Africa. Washkanski had his operation on this date.

3 December 1984
Bhopal is in India. The accident happened on this date.

4 December 1154
Nicholas Breakspear, who became Pope on this date, was English.

4 December 1872
The *Mary Celeste*, which was found abandoned on this date.

4 December 1937
The *Dandy*.

5 December 1594
Gerhard Kramer (Gerardus Mercator), who died on this date, made maps.

5 December 1791
W. A. Mozart, who died on this date.

5 December 1839
Gen. George Custer, who was born on this date.

5 December 1933
To buy, sell or drink alcohol. Prohibition was lifted on this date. All it did was make criminals out of ordinary people and millionaires out of gangsters.

5 December 1979
Jack Lynch.

6 December 1921
In London, on this date.

6 December 1946
José Carreras, who was born on this date, resumed his career after fighting leukaemia.

6 December 1988
Roy Orbison, who died on this date.

7 December 1817
Capt. William Bligh, who died on this date.

7 December 1941
The Japanese attacked Pearl Harbor, Hawaii, on this date.

7 December 1988
Armenia suffered a severe earthquake on this date.

7 December 1991
Dubrovnik was bombed on this date.

8 December 1542
Mary Queen of Scots, who was beheaded on this date. It was Queen Elizabeth who signed her death warrant.

8 December 1980
John Lennon, who was murdered on this date.

9 December 1967
Nicolae Ceausescu became President of Romania on this date.

9 December 1990
Lech Walesa was elected President of Poland on this date.

10 December 1830
Emily Dickinson, who was born on this date, was American.

10 December 1896
Alfred Nobel, who died on this date.

11 December 1905
Erskine Childers.

11 December 1918
Russia. He was born on this date.

11 December 1936
He gave up the throne on this date.

11 December 1979
Charles Haughey was confirmed Taoiseach on this date.

12 December 1913
The *Mona Lisa*, which was recovered on this date.

12 December 1915
Frank Sinatra, who was born on this date.

12 December 1946
Emerson Fittipaldi, who was born on this date in Brazil, was a world champion motorist.

12 December 1955
The hovercraft.

13 December 1925
Chitty Chitty Bang Bang. Dick van Dyke was born on this date.

13 December 1929
Christopher Plummer, who was born on this date, starred in *The Sound of Music*.

14 December 1911
Amundsen, who reached the South Pole on this date, left a note for Capt. Robert Scott, who was also trying to reach the South Pole.

15 December 1832
Gustave Eiffel, who was born on this date.

15 December 1840
Napoleon Bonaparte, who was buried in Paris on this date.

15 December 1890
Sitting Bull.

15 December 1892
Oil. Getty was born on this date.

16 December 1770
Ludwig van Beethoven, who was born on this date.

16 December 1773
In Boston. The so-called Boston Tea Party happened on this date.

16 December 1944
Glen Miller, who went missing on this date.

17 December 1778
Sir Humphry Davy, who was born on this date.

17 December 1857
Sir Francis Beaufort died on this date.

17 December 1903
The Wright brothers, who made their first flight on this date.

18 December 1737
Antonio Stradivari died on this date.

18 December 1779
Joe Grimaldi, who was born on this date.

18 December 1919
Alcock, one of the first people to fly the Atlantic, died in an air crash on this date.

18 December 1947
Tyrannosaurus rex. Steven Spielberg was born on this date.

19 December 1923
Gordon Jackson, who was born on this date.

20 December 1952
Jenny Agutter, who was born on this date, did not appear in *Cabaret*.

20 December 1968
John Steinbeck, who died on this date.

21 December 1620
Massachusetts. The Pilgrim Fathers landed on this date.

21 December 1935
Walt Disney Studios produced *Snow White*, which had its première on this date.

21 December 1940
F. Scott Fitzgerald, who died on this date.

21 December 1945
Gen. Patton was killed in a car crash on this date.

21 December 1968
A person flew around the Moon before landing on it. Astronauts Borman, Lovell and Anders were the first to do this, in a mission that was launched on this date.

21 December 1991
Jane Fonda married Ted Turner on this date.

22 December 1988
The doomed jet that exploded over Lockerbie on this date belonged to Pan-American Airways.

23 December 1888
Vincent van Gogh cut off his earlobe on this date.

23 December 1912
Karsh of Ottawa, who was born on this date, uses his camera for his famous portraits.

24 December 1491
Loyola, who was born on this date, was Spanish.

24 December 1601
At the Battle of Kinsale on this date.

24 December 1871
Giuseppe Verdi. The opera opened in Cairo's new opera house on this date.

25 December 4 BC
Jesus Christ. Historians matching other events to the life of Jesus are confident that the date of birth fell in what we call 4 BC. The date of 25 December, however, is a later tradition.

25 December 1889
Humphrey Bogart, who was born on this date.

25 December 1977
The body of Charlie Chaplin, who died on this date, was stolen by fortune hunters. It was later recovered.

25 December 1989
Nicolae Ceausescu and his wife, Elena, were shot by firing squad in Romania on this date.

26 December 1831
Charles Darwin. The voyage of the *Beagle* began on this date.

26 December 1972
Harry Truman, who died on this date, became president in 1945 on the death of Franklin Roosevelt.

26 December 1989
Samuel Beckett, who died on this date, usually wrote in French.

27 December 1904
The Abbey Theatre opened on this date.

27 December 1983
Pope John Paul II paid a visit to his would-be killer on this date.

28 December 1732
A real person. Roibeard Ruadh MacGreagòir (Rob Roy Macgregor) was a Scottish outlaw. Scott died on this date.

28 December 1949
Albert Einstein made the comment on this date.

29 December 1170 (a)
St Thomas Becket was murdered in Canterbury Cathedral on this date.

29 December 1170 (b)
T. S. Eliot. (See the previous answer.)

29 December 1986
Macmillan, who died on this date, was a Conservative.

30 December 1916
Grigori Rasputin, who was murdered on this date.

30 December 1979
Richard Rogers, who died on this date, was the music writer.

31 December 1943
Ben Kingsley, who was born on this date, played the role of Mohandas (Mahatma) Gandhi.

A crash course in Roman numerals

I	means 1
II	means 2
III	means 3
IV	(an I before a V) means 4
V	means 5
VI	(an I after a V) means 6
VII	means 7
VIII	means 8
IX	(an I before an X) means 9
X	means 10
XI	means 11 (and so on)

So, in the low numbers, it is simply I for units, V for 5 units, and X for 10 units. Having a letter before a higher letter means you subtract it, and after a higher letter you add it. So King Louis XIV of France is Louis the fourteenth (X + IV = 10 + 4 = 14). Are you getting the hang of it?

These rules break down a little bit with very high numbers. But relax. All you need for this book is 23, for Pope John XXIII (the twenty-third).

Perpetual Calendar, 1801-2000

[i] Years		[ii] Months											
1801–1900	**1901–2000**	**J**	**F**	**M**	**A**	**M**	**J**	**J**	**A**	**S**	**O**	**N**	**D**
01 29 57 85	25 53 81	4	0	0	3	5	1	3	6	2	4	0	2
02 30 58 86	26 54 82	5	1	1	4	6	2	4	0	3	5	1	3
03 31 59 87	27 55 83	6	2	2	5	0	3	5	1	4	6	2	4
04 32 60 88	28 56 84	0	3	4	0	2	5	0	3	6	1	4	6
05 33 61 89	01 29 57 85	2	5	5	1	3	6	1	4	0	2	5	0
06 34 62 90	02 30 58 86	3	6	6	2	4	0	2	5	1	3	6	1
07 35 63 91	03 31 59 87	4	0	0	3	5	1	3	6	2	4	0	2
08 36 64 92	04 32 60 88	5	1	2	5	0	3	5	1	4	6	2	4
09 37 65 93	05 33 61 89	0	3	3	6	1	4	6	2	5	0	3	5
10 38 66 94	06 34 62 90	1	4	4	0	2	5	0	3	6	1	4	6
11 39 67 95	07 35 63 91	2	5	5	1	3	6	1	4	0	2	5	0
12 40 68 96	08 36 64 92	3	6	0	3	5	1	3	6	2	4	0	2
13 41 69 97	09 37 65 93	5	1	1	4	6	2	4	0	3	5	1	3
14 42 70 98	10 38 66 94	6	2	2	5	0	3	5	1	4	6	2	4
15 43 71 99	11 39 67 95	0	3	3	6	1	4	6	2	5	0	3	5
16 44 72	12 40 68 96	1	4	5	1	3	6	1	4	0	2	5	0
17 45 73	13 41 69 97	3	6	6	2	4	0	2	5	1	3	6	1
18 46 74	14 42 70 98	4	0	0	3	5	1	3	6	2	4	0	2
19 47 75	15 43 71 99	5	1	1	4	6	2	4	0	3	5	1	3
20 48 76	16 44 72	6	2	3	6	1	4	6	2	5	0	3	5
21 49 77 00	17 45 73	1	4	4	0	2	5	0	3	6	1	4	6
22 50 78	18 46 74	2	5	5	1	3	6	1	4	0	2	5	0
23 51 79	19 47 75	3	6	6	2	4	0	2	5	1	3	6	1
24 52 80	20 48 76	4	0	1	4	6	2	4	0	3	5	1	3
25 53 81	21 49 77 00	6	2	2	5	0	3	5	1	4	6	2	4
26 54 82	22 50 78	0	3	3	6	1	4	6	2	5	0	3	5
27 55 83	23 51 79	1	4	4	0	2	5	0	3	6	1	4	6
28 56 84	24 52 80	2	5	6	2	4	0	2	5	1	3	6	1

Example:

WHICH DAY OF THE WEEK WAS
24 MAY 1957?

Find the year in group i, and follow the horizontal line until you find the month in group ii. Add this number (3) to the number of the day (24); the total (27), when found in group iii, shows that 24 May 1957 was a Friday.

[iii]	Days of the week					
Sun	1	8	15	22	29	36
Mon	2	9	16	23	30	37
Tue	3	10	17	24	31	
Wed	4	11	18	25	32	
Thu	5	12	19	26	33	
Fri	6	13	20	27	34	
Sat	7	14	21	28	35	